THE MIRACLE WORKER

"The story of Annie Sullivan, the slum-bred, once-blind girl who tamed the young animal that was the blind, deaf and mute child, Helen Keller. Radiant, emotion-charged, memorable, superb!"

Philadelphia Inquirer

"Really and truly powerful, hair-raising, spine-tingling, touching and just plain wonderful!"

New York Herald Tribune

THE ACTOR'S SCENEBOOK edited by Michael Schulman and
   Eva Mekler
THE ACTOR'S SCENEBOOK II edited by Michael Schulman
   and Eva Mekler
AUDITION by Michael Shurtleff
BRIAN'S SONG by William Blinn
THE EFFECT OF GAMMA RAYS ON MAN IN THE MOON
   MARIGOLDS by Paul Zindel
50 GREAT SCENES FOR STUDENT ACTORS edited by
   Lewy Olfson
FILM SCENES FOR ACTORS edited by Joshua Karton
FILM SCENES FOR ACTORS II edited by Joshua Karton
FOOL FOR LOVE & OTHER PLAYS by Sam Shepard
FOUR GREAT PLAYS by Henrik Ibsen
FIVE MAJOR PLAYS by Anton Chekhov
FOR COLORED GIRLS WHO HAVE CONSIDERED SUICIDE
   WHEN THE RAINBOW IS ENUF by Ntozake Shange
INHERIT THE WIND by Jerome Lawrence and Robert E. Lee
THE MIRACLE WORKER by William Gibson
MODERN AMERICAN SCENES FOR STUDENT ACTORS
   edited by Wynn Handman
THE MOUSETRAP AND OTHER PLAYS by Agatha Christie
THE NIGHT THOREAU SPENT IN JAIL by Jerome Lawrence
   and Robert E. Lee
SAM SHEPARD: SEVEN PLAYS by Sam Shepard
THE TECHNIQUE OF ACTING by Stella Adler
THE UNSEEN HAND AND OTHER PLAYS by Sam Shepard

THE MIRACLE WORKER

BY WILLIAM GIBSON

BANTAM BOOKS

NEW YORK · TORONTO · LONDON · SYDNEY · AUCKLAND

RL 5, IL 12+

THE MIRACLE WORKER

*A Bantam Book / published by arrangement with
Atheneum House, Inc.*

PRINTING HISTORY

Atheneum edition published October 1960

Fireside Theater Club edition published April 1961

Bantam edition / May 1962

Bantam Pathfinder edition / May 1964

Bantam edition / July 1975

ISBN 0-553-24778-6

Published simultaneously in the United States and Canada

---

*Bantam Books are published by Bantam Books, a division of Bantam
Doubleday Dell Publishing Group, Inc. Its trademark, consisting of the
words "Bantam Books" and the portrayal of a rooster, is Registered in U.S.
Patent and Trademark Office and in other countries. Marca Registrada.
Bantam Books, 666 Fifth Avenue, New York, New York 10103.*

PRINTED IN THE UNITED STATES OF AMERICA

RAD   52 51 50 49

for the wife and the kids and the next breath
with love

———————————

THE MIRACLE WORKER

A PLAY IN THREE ACTS

"At another time she asked, 'What is a soul?' 'No one knows,' I replied; 'but we know it is not the body, and it is that part of us which thinks and loves and hopes.' . . . [and] is invisible. . . . 'But if I write what my soul thinks,' she said, 'then it will be visible, and the words will be its body.'"

—ANNIE SULLIVAN, 1891

THE PLAYING SPACE *is divided into two areas by a more or less diagonal line, which runs from downstage right to upstage left.*

THE AREA *behind this diagonal is on platforms and represents the Keller house; inside we see, down right, a family room, and up center, elevated, a bedroom. On stage level near center, outside a porch, there is a water pump.*

THE OTHER AREA, *in front of the diagonal, is neutral ground; it accommodates various places as designated at various times—the yard before the Keller home, the Perkins Institution for the Blind, the garden house, and so forth.*

THE CONVENTION OF THE STAGING *is one of cutting through time and place, and its essential qualities are fluidity and spatial counterpoint. To this end, the less set there is, the better; in a literal set, the fluidity will seem merely episodic. The stage therefore should be free, airy, unencumbered by walls. Apart from certain practical items—such as the pump, a window to climb out of, doors to be locked—locales should be only skeletal suggestions, and the movement from one to another should be accomplishable by little more than lights.*

CHARACTERS

A DOCTOR

KATE

KELLER

HELEN

MARTHA

PERCY

AUNT EV

JAMES

ANAGNOS

ANNIE SULLIVAN

VINEY

BLIND GIRLS

A SERVANT

OFFSTAGE VOICES

TIME: *The 1880's.*

PLACE: *In and around the Keller homestead in Tus-
cumbia, Alabama; also, briefly, the Perkins Institution
for the Blind, in Boston.*

ACT I

IT IS NIGHT OVER THE KELLER HOMESTEAD.

Inside, three adults in the bedroom are grouped around a crib, in lamplight. They have been through a long vigil, and it shows in their tired bearing and disarranged clothing. One is a young gentlewoman with a sweet girlish face, KATE KELLER; *the second is an elderly* DOCTOR, *stethoscope at neck, thermometer in fingers; the third is a hearty gentleman in his forties with chin whiskers,* CAPTAIN ARTHUR KELLER.

DOCTOR: She'll live.

KATE: Thank God.

> (*The* DOCTOR *leaves them together over the crib, packs his bag.*)

DOCTOR: You're a pair of lucky parents. I can tell you now, I thought she wouldn't.

KELLER: Nonsense, the child's a Keller, she has the constitution of a goat. She'll outlive us all.

DOCTOR [AMIABLY]: Yes, especially if some of you Kellers don't get a night's sleep. I mean you, Mrs. Keller.

KELLER: You hear, Katie?

KATE: I hear.

KELLER [INDULGENT]: I've brought up two of them, but this is my wife's first, she isn't battle-scarred yet.

KATE: Doctor, don't be merely considerate, will my girl be all right?

DOCTOR: Oh, by morning she'll be knocking down Captain Keller's fences again.

KATE: And isn't there anything we should do?

KELLER [JOVIAL]: Put up stronger fencing, ha?

DOCTOR: Just let her get well, she knows how to do it better than we do.

(*He is packed, ready to leave.*)

Main thing is the fever's gone, these things come and go in infants, never know why. Call it acute congestion of the stomach and brain.

KELLER: I'll see you to your buggy, Doctor.

DOCTOR: I've never seen a baby, more vitality, that's the truth.

(*He beams a good night at the baby and* KATE, *and* KELLER *leads him downstairs with a lamp. They go down the porch steps, and across the yard, where the* DOCTOR *goes off left;* KELLER *stands with the lamp aloft.* KATE *meanwhile is bent lovingly over the crib, which emits a bleat; her finger is playful with the baby's face.*)

KATE: Hush. Don't you cry now, you've been trouble enough. Call it acute congestion, indeed, I don't see what's so cute about a congestion, just because it's yours. We'll have your father run an editorial in his paper, the wonders of modern medicine, they don't know what they're curing even when they cure it. Men, men and their battle scars, we women will have to—

(*But she breaks off, puzzled, moves her finger before the baby's eyes.*)

Will have to—Helen?

(*Now she moves her hand, quickly.*)

Helen.

(*She snaps her fingers at the baby's eyes twice, and*

her hand falters; after a moment she calls out, loudly.)

Captain. Captain, will you come—

(But she stares at the baby, and her next call is directly at her ears.)

Captain!

(And now, still staring, KATE screams. KELLER in the yard hears it, and runs with the lamp back to the house. KATE screams again, her look intent on the baby and terrible. KELLER hurries in and up.)

KELLER: Katie? What's wrong?
KATE: Look.

(She makes a pass with her hand in the crib, at the baby's eyes.)

KELLER: What, Katie? She's well, she needs only time to—
KATE: She can't see. Look at her eyes.

(She takes the lamp from him, moves it before the child's face.)

She can't see!
KELLER [HOARSELY]: Helen.
KATE: Or hear. When I screamed she didn't blink. Not an eyelash—
KELLER: Helen. Helen!
KATE: She can't *hear* you!
KELLER: *Helen!*

(His face has something like fury in it, crying the child's name; KATE almost fainting presses her knuckles to her mouth, to stop her own cry.

The room dims out quickly.

Time, in the form of a slow tune of distant belfry chimes which approaches in a crescendo and then fades, passes; the light comes up again on a day five years later, on three kneeling children and an old dog outside around the pump.

The dog is a setter named BELLE, *and she is sleeping. Two of the children are Negroes,* MARTHA *and* PERCY. *The third child is* HELEN, *six and a half years old, quite unkempt, in body a vivacious little person with a fine head, attractive, but noticeably blind, one eye larger and protruding; her gestures are abrupt, insistent, lacking in human restraint, and her face never smiles. She is flanked by the other two, in a litter of paper-doll cutouts, and while they speak* HELEN'S *hands thrust at their faces in turn, feeling baffledly at the movements of their lips.*)

MARTHA [SNIPPING]: First I'm gonna cut off this doctor's legs, one, two, now then—
PERCY: Why you cuttin' off that doctor's legs?
MARTHA: I'm gonna give him a operation. Now I'm gonna cut off his arms, one, two. Now I'm gonna fix up—

(*She pushes* HELEN'S *hand away from her mouth.*)

You stop that.
PERCY: Cut off his stomach, that's a good operation.
MARTHA: No, I'm gonna cut off his head first, he got a bad cold.
PERCY: Ain't gonna be much of that doctor left to fix up, time you finish all them opera—

(*But* HELEN *is poking her fingers inside his mouth, to feel his tongue; he bites at them, annoyed, and*

*she jerks them away. HELEN now fingers her own
lips, moving them in imitation, but soundlessly.)*

MARTHA: What you do, bite her hand?

PERCY: That's how I do, she keep pokin' her fingers in
my mouth, I just bite 'em off.

MARTHA: What she tryin' do now?

PERCY: She tryin' *talk*. She gonna get mad. Looka her
tryin' talk.

*(HELEN is scowling, the lips under her fingertips
moving in ghostly silence, growing more and more
frantic, until in a bizarre rage she bites at her own
fingers. This sends PERCY off into laughter, but alarms
MARTHA.)*

MARTHA: Hey, you stop now.

(She pulls HELEN's hand down.)

You just sit quiet and—

*(But at once HELEN topples MARTHA on her back,
knees pinning her shoulders down, and grabs the
scissors. MARTHA screams. PERCY darts to the bell
string on the porch, yanks it, and the bell rings.*

*Inside, the lights have been gradually coming up on
the main room, where we see the family informally
gathered, talking, but in pantomime: KATE sits darn-
ing socks near a cradle, occasionally rocking it; CAP-
TAIN KELLER in spectacles is working over newspaper
pages at a table; a benign visitor in a hat, AUNT EV, is
sharing the sewing basket, putting the finishing touches
on a big shapeless doll made out of towels; an indolent
young man, JAMES KELLER, is at the window watching
the children.*

With the ring of the bell, KATE is instantly on her

*feet and out the door onto the porch, to take in the
scene; now we see what these five years have done to
her, the girlish playfulness is gone, she is a woman
steeled in grief.)*

KATE [FOR THE THOUSANDTH TIME]: Helen.

*(She is down the steps at once to them, seizing
HELEN's wrists and lifting her off MARTHA; MARTHA
runs off in tears and screams for momma, with PERCY
after her.)*

Let me have those scissors.

*(Meanwhile the family inside is alerted, AUNT EV join-
ing JAMES at the window; CAPTAIN KELLER resumes
work.)*

JAMES [BLANDLY]:. She only dug Martha's eyes out. Almost dug. It's always almost, no point worrying till
it happens, is there?

*(They gaze out, while KATE reaches for the scissors
in HELEN's hand. But HELEN pulls the scissors back,
they struggle for them a moment, then KATE gives up,
lets HELEN keep them. She tries to draw HELEN into
the house. HELEN jerks away. KATE next goes down on
her knees, takes HELEN's hands gently, and using the
scissors like a doll, makes HELEN caress and cradle
them; she points HELEN's finger housewards. HELEN's
whole body now becomes eager; she surrenders the
scissors, KATE turns her toward the door and gives
her a little push. HELEN scrambles up and toward the
house, and KATE rising follows her.)*

AUNT EV: How does she stand it? Why haven't you seen
this Baltimore man? It's not a thing you can let go
on and on, like the weather.

JAMES: The weather here doesn't ask permission of me, Aunt Ev. Speak to my father.

AUNT EV: Arthur. Something ought to be done for that child.

KELLER: A refreshing suggestion. What?

(KATE *entering turns* HELEN *to* AUNT EV, *who gives her the towel doll.*)

AUNT EV: Why, this very famous oculist in Baltimore I wrote you about, what was his name?

KATE: Dr. Chisholm.

AUNT EV: Yes, I heard lots of cases of blindness people thought couldn't be cured he's cured, he just does wonders. Why don't you write to him?

KELLER: I've stopped believing in wonders.

KATE [ROCKS THE CRADLE]: I think the Captain will write to him soon. Won't you, Captain?

KELLER: No.

JAMES [LIGHTLY]: Good money after bad, or bad after good. Or bad after bad—

AUNT EV: Well, if it's just a question of money, Arthur, now you're marshal you have this Yankee money. Might as well—

KELLER: Not money. The child's been to specialists all over Alabama and Tennessee, if I thought it would do good I'd have her to every fool doctor in the country.

KATE: I think the Captain will write to him soon.

KELLER: Katie. How many times can you let them break your heart?

KATE: Any number of times.

(HELEN *meanwhile sits on the floor to explore the doll with her fingers, and her hand pauses over the face: this is no face, a blank area of towel, and it troubles her. Her hand searches for features, and taps ques-*

*tioningly for eyes, but no one notices. She then yanks
at her* AUNT'S *dress, and taps again vigorously for
eyes.)*

AUNT EV: What, child?

(Obviously not hearing, HELEN *commences to go
around, from person to person, tapping for eyes, but
no one attends or understands.)*

KATE [NO BREAK]: As long as there's the least chance.
For her to see. Or hear, or—
KELLER: There isn't. Now I must finish here.
KATE: I think, with your permission, Captain, I'd like to
write.
KELLER: I said no, Katie.
AUNT EV: Why, writing does no harm, Arthur, only a little
bitty letter. To see if he can help her.
KELLER: He can't.
KATE: We won't know that to be a fact, Captain, until
after you write.
KELLER [RISING, EMPHATIC]: Katie, he can't.

(He collects his papers.)

JAMES [FACETIOUSLY]: Father stands up, that makes it
a fact.
KELLER: You be quiet! I'm badgered enough here by
females without your impudence.

*(*JAMES *shuts up, makes himself scarce.* HELEN *now
is groping among things on* KELLER'S *desk, and paws
his papers to the floor.* KELLER *is exasperated.)*

Katie.

*(*KATE *quickly turns* HELEN *away, and retrieves the
papers.)*

I might as well try to work in a henyard as in this
house—

JAMES [PLACATING]: You really ought to put her away,
Father.

KATE [STARING UP]: What?

JAMES: Some asylum. It's the kindest thing.

AUNT EV: Why, she's your sister, James, not a nobody—

JAMES: Half sister, and half—mentally defective, she can't
even keep herself clean. It's not pleasant to see her
about all the time.

KATE: Do you dare? Complain of what you *can* see?

KELLER [VERY ANNOYED]: This discussion is at an end!
I'll thank you not to broach it again, Ev.

(*Silence descends at once.* HELEN *gropes her way
with the doll, and* KELLER *turns back for a final word,
explosive.*)

I've done as much as I can bear, I can't give my whole
life to it! The house is at sixes and sevens from morning till night over the child, it's time some attention
was paid to Mildred here instead!

KATE [GENTLY DRY]: You'll wake her up, Captain.

KELLER: I want some peace in the house, I don't care
how, but one way we won't have it is by rushing up
and down the country every time someone hears of a
new quack. I'm as sensible to this affliction as anyone
else, it hurts me to look at the girl.

KATE: It was not our affliction I meant you to write about,
Captain.

(HELEN *is back at* AUNT EV, *fingering her dress, and
yanks two buttons from it.*)

AUNT EV: Helen! My buttons.

(HELEN *pushes the buttons into the doll's face.* KATE
now sees, comes swiftly to kneel, lifts HELEN's *hand
to her own eyes in question.*)

KATE: Eyes?

(HELEN *nods energetically.*)

She wants the doll to have eyes.

(*Another kind of silence now, while* KATE *takes pins
and buttons from the sewing basket and attaches them
to the doll as eyes.* KELLER *stands, caught, and watches
morosely.* AUNT EV *blinks, and conceals her emotion
by inspecting her dress.*)

AUNT EV: My goodness me, I'm not decent.
KATE: She doesn't know better, Aunt Ev. I'll sew them
on again.
JAMES: Never learn with everyone letting her do any-
thing she takes it into her mind to—
KELLER: You be quiet!
JAMES: What did I say now?
KELLER: You talk too much.
JAMES: I was agreeing with you!
KELLER: Whatever it was. Deprived child, the least she
can have are the little things she wants.

(JAMES, *very wounded, stalks out of the room onto
the porch; he remains here, sulking.*)

AUNT EV [INDULGENTLY]: It's worth a couple of buttons,
Kate, look.

(HELEN *now has the doll with eyes, and cannot con-
tain herself for joy; she rocks the doll, pats it vigorously, kisses it.*)

This child has more sense than all these men Kellers,
if there's ever any way to reach that mind of hers.

(*But* HELEN *suddenly has come upon the cradle, and
unhesitatingly overturns it; the swaddled baby tumbles*

out, and CAPTAIN KELLER *barely manages to dive and
catch it in time.)*

KELLER: *Helen!*

(All are in commotion, the baby screams, but HELEN
unperturbed is laying her doll in its place. KATE *on her
knees pulls her hands off the cradle, wringing them;*
HELEN *is bewildered.)*

KATE: Helen, Helen, you're not to do such things, how
can I make you understand—

KELLER [HOARSELY]: Katie.

KATE: How can I get it into your head, my darling, my
poor—

KELLER: Katie, some way of teaching her an iota of discipline has to be—

KATE [FLARING]: How can you discipline an afflicted
child? Is it her fault?

*(*HELEN's *fingers have fluttered to her* MOTHER's *lips,
vainly trying to comprehend their movements.)*

KELLER: I didn't say it was her fault.

KATE: Then whose? I don't know what to do! How can
I teach her, beat her—until she's black and blue?

KELLER: It's not safe to let her run around loose. Now
there must be a way of confining her, somehow, so
she can't—

KATE: Where, in a cage? She's a growing child, she has
to use her limbs!

KELLER: Answer me one thing, is it fair to Mildred here?

KATE [INEXORABLY]: Are you willing to put her away?

(Now HELEN's *face darkens in the same rage as at
herself earlier, and her hand strikes at* KATE's *lips.*
KATE *catches her hand again, and* HELEN *begins to
kick, struggle, twist.)*

KELLER: Now what?

KATE: She wants to talk, like—*be* like you and me.

(*She holds* HELEN *struggling until we hear from the child her first sound so far, an inarticulate weird noise in her throat such as an animal in a trap might make; and* KATE *releases her. The second she is free* HELEN *blunders away, collides violently with a chair, falls, and sits weeping.* KATE *comes to her, embraces, caresses, soothes her, and buries her own face in her hair, until she can control her voice.*)

Every day she slips further away. And I don't know how to call her back.

AUNT EV: Oh, I've a mind to take her up to Baltimore myself. If that doctor can't help her, maybe he'll know who can.

KELLER [PRESENTLY, HEAVILY]: I'll write the man, Katie.

(*He stands with the baby in his clasp, staring at* HELEN'S *head, hanging down on* KATE'S *arm.*

The lights dim out, except the one on KATE *and* HELEN. *In the twilight,* JAMES, AUNT EV, *and* KELLER *move off slowly, formally, in separate directions;* KATE *with* HELEN *in her arms remains, motionless, in an image which overlaps into the next scene and fades only when it is well under way.*

Without pause, from the dark down left we hear a man's voice with a Greek accent speaking:)

ANAGNOS: —who could do nothing for the girl, of course. It was Dr. Bell who thought she might somehow be taught. I have written the family only that a suitable governess, Miss Annie Sullivan, has been found here in Boston—

(*The lights begin to come up, down left, on a long*

table and chair. The table contains equipment for teaching the blind by touch—a small replica of the human skeleton, stuffed animals, models of flowers and plants, piles of books. The chair contains a girl of 20, ANNIE SULLIVAN, with a face which in repose is grave and rather obstinate, and when active is impudent, combative, twinkling with all the life that is lacking in HELEN'S, and handsome; there is a crude vitality to her. Her suitcase is at her knee. ANAGNOS, a stocky bearded man, comes into the light only towards the end of his speech.)

ANAGNOS: —and will come. It will no doubt be difficult for you there, Annie. But it has been difficult for you at our school too, hm? Gratifying, yes, when you came to us and could not spell your name, to accomplish so much here in a few years, but always an Irish battle. For independence.

(He studies ANNIE, humorously; she does not open her eyes.)

This is my last time to counsel you, Annie, and you do lack some—by some I mean *all*—what, tact or talent to bend. To others. And what has saved you on more than one occasion here at Perkins is that there was nowhere to expel you to. Your eyes hurt?

ANNIE: My ears, Mr. Anagnos.

(And now she has opened her eyes; they are inflamed, vague, slightly crossed, clouded by the granular growth of trachoma, and she often keeps them closed to shut out the pain of light.)

ANAGNOS [SEVERELY]: Nowhere but back to Tewksbury, where children learn to be saucy. Annie, I know how dreadful it was there, but that battle is dead and done with, why not let it stay buried?

ANNIE [CHEERILY]: I think God must owe me a resurrection.

ANAGNOS [A BIT SHOCKED]: What?

ANNIE [TAPS HER BROW]: Well, He keeps digging up that battle!

ANAGNOS: That is not a proper thing to say, Annie. It is what I mean.

ANNIE [MEEKLY]: Yes. But I know what I'm like, what's this child like?

ANAGNOS: Like?

ANNIE: Well— Bright or dull, to start off.

ANAGNOS: No one knows. And if she is dull, you have no patience with this?

ANNIE: Oh, in grownups you have to, Mr. Anagnos. I mean in children it just seems a little—precocious, can I use that word?

ANAGNOS: Only if you can spell it.

ANNIE: Premature. So I hope at least she's a bright one.

ANAGNOS: Deaf, blind, mute—who knows? She is like a little safe, locked, that no one can open. Perhaps there is a treasure inside.

ANNIE: Maybe it's empty, too?

ANAGNOS: Possible. I should warn you, she is much given to tantrums.

ANNIE: Means something is inside. Well, so am I, if I believe all I hear. Maybe you should warn *them*.

ANAGNOS [FROWNS]: Annie. I wrote them no word of your history. You will find yourself among strangers now, who know nothing of it.

ANNIE: Well, we'll keep them in a state of blessed ignorance.

ANAGNOS: Perhaps *you* should tell it?

ANNIE [BRISTLING]: Why? I have enough trouble with people who don't know.

ANAGNOS: So they will understand. When you have trouble.

ANNIE: The only time I have trouble is when I'm right.

(*But she is amused at herself, as is* ANAGNOS.)

Is it my fault it's so often? I won't give them trouble,
Mr. Anagnos, I'll be so ladylike they won't notice
I've come.

ANAGNOS: Annie, be—humble. It is not as if you have so
many offers to pick and choose. You will need their
affection, working with this child.

ANNIE [HUMOROUSLY]: I hope I won't need their pity.

ANAGNOS: Oh, we can all use some pity.

(*Crisply*)

So. You are no longer our pupil, we throw you into
the world, a teacher. *If* the child can be taught. No
one expects you to work miracles, even for twenty-
five dollars a month. Now, in this envelope a loan,
for the railroad, which you will repay me when you
have a bank account. But in this box, a gift. With
our love.

(ANNIE *opens the small box he extends, and sees a
garnet ring. She looks up, blinking, and down.*)

I think other friends are ready to say goodbye.

(*He moves as though to open doors.*)

ANNIE: Mr. Anagnos.

(*Her voice is trembling.*)

Dear Mr. Anagnos, I—

(*But she swallows over getting the ring on her finger,
and cannot continue until she finds a woebegone
joke.*)

Well, what should I say, I'm an ignorant opinionated
girl, and everything I am I owe to you?

ANAGNOS [SMILES]: That is only half true, Annie.

ANNIE: Which half? I crawled in here like a drowned rat,
I thought I died when Jimmie died, that I'd never
again—come alive. Well, you say with love so easy,
and I haven't *loved* a soul since and I never will, I
suppose, but this place gave me more than my eyes
back. Or taught me how to spell, which I'll never
learn anyway, but with all the fights and the trouble
I've been here it taught me what help is, and how to
live again, and I don't want to say goodbye. Don't
open the door, I'm crying.

ANAGNOS [GENTLY]: They will not see.

(*He moves again as though opening doors, and in
comes a group of girls, 8-year-olds to 17-year-olds; as
they walk we see they are blind.* ANAGNOS *shepherds
them in with a hand.*)

A CHILD: Annie?

ANNIE [HER VOICE CHEERFUL]: Here, Beatrice.

(*As soon as they locate her voice they throng joyfully
to her, speaking all at once;* ANNIE *is down on her
knees to the smallest, and the following are the more
intelligible fragments in the general hubbub.*)

CHILDREN: There's a present. We brought you a going-
away present, Annie!

ANNIE: Oh, now you shouldn't have—

CHILDREN: We did, we did, where's the present?

SMALLEST CHILD [MOURNFULLY]: Don't go, Annie, away.

CHILDREN: Alice has it. Alice! Where's Alice? Here I am!
Where? Here!

(*An arm is aloft out of the group, waving a present;*
ANNIE *reaches for it.*)

ANNIE: I have it. I have it, everybody, should I open it?

CHILDREN: Open it! Everyone be quiet! Do, Annie! She's
opening it. Ssh!

(*A settling of silence while* ANNIE *unwraps it. The present is a pair of smoked glasses, and she stands still.*)

Is it open, Annie?

ANNIE: It's open.

CHILDREN: It's for your eyes, Annie. Put them on, Annie! 'Cause Mrs. Hopkins said your eyes hurt since the operation. And she said you're going where the sun is *fierce*.

ANNIE: I'm putting them on now.

SMALLEST CHILD [MOURNFULLY]: Don't go, Annie, where the sun is fierce.

CHILDREN: Do they fit all right?

ANNIE: Oh, they fit just fine.

CHILDREN: Did you put them on? Are they pretty, Annie?

ANNIE: Oh, my eyes feel hundreds of per cent better already, and pretty, why, do you know how I look in them? Splendiloquent. Like a race horse!

CHILDREN [DELIGHTED]: There's another present! Beatrice! We have a present for Helen, too! Give it to her, Beatrice. Here, Annie!

(*This present is an elegant doll, with movable eyelids and a momma sound.*)

It's for Helen. And we took up a collection to buy it. And Laura dressed it.

ANNIE: It's beautiful!

CHILDREN: So don't forget, you be sure to give it to Helen from us, Annie!

ANNIE: I promise it will be the first thing I give her. If I don't keep it for myself, that is, you know I can't be trusted with dolls!

SMALLEST CHILD [MOURNFULLY]: Don't go, Annie, to her.

ANNIE [HER ARM AROUND HER]: Sarah, dear. I don't *want* to go.

SMALLEST CHILD: Then why are you going?

ANNIE [GENTLY]: Because I'm a big girl now, and big
girls have to earn a living. It's the only way I can.
But if you don't smile for me first, what I'll just have
to do is—

(*She pauses, inviting it.*)

SMALLEST CHILD: What?
ANNIE: Put *you* in my suitcase, instead of this doll. And
take *you* to Helen in Alabama!

(*This strikes the children as very funny, and they
begin to laugh and tease the smallest child, who after
a moment does smile for* ANNIE.)

ANAGNOS [THEN]: Come, children. We must get the trunk
into the carriage and Annie into her train, or no one
will go to Alabama. Come, come.

(*He shepherds them out and* ANNIE *is left alone on
her knees with the doll in her lap. She reaches for
her suitcase, and by a subtle change in the color of
the light, we go with her thoughts into another time.
We hear a boy's voice whispering; perhaps we see
shadowy intimations of these speakers in the background.*)

BOY'S VOICE: Where we goin', Annie?
ANNIE [IN DREAD]: Jimmie.
BOY'S VOICE: Where we goin'?
ANNIE: I said—I'm takin' care of you—
BOY'S VOICE: Forever and ever?
MAN'S VOICE [IMPERSONAL]: Annie Sullivan, aged nine,
virtually blind. James Sullivan, aged seven—What's the
matter with your leg, Sonny?
ANNIE: Forever and ever.
MAN'S VOICE: Can't he walk without that crutch?

(ANNIE *shakes her head, and does not stop shaking it.*)

Girl goes to the women's ward. Boy to the men's.

BOY'S VOICE [IN TERROR]: Annie! Annie, don't let them take me—Annie!

ANAGNOS [OFFSTAGE]: Annie! Annie?

(*But this voice is real, in the present, and* ANNIE *comes up out of her horror, clearing her head with a final shake; the lights begin to pick out* KATE *in the* KELLER *house, as* ANNIE *in a bright tone calls back.*)

ANNIE: Coming!

(*This word catches* KATE, *who stands half turned and attentive to it, almost as though hearing it. Meanwhile* ANNIE *turns and hurries out, lugging the suitcase.*

The room dims out; the sound of railroad wheels begins from off left, and maintains itself in a constant rhythm underneath the following scene; the remaining lights have come up on the KELLER *homestead.* JAMES *is lounging on the porch, waiting. In the upper bedroom which is to be* ANNIE'S, HELEN *is alone, puzzledly exploring, fingering and smelling things, the curtains, empty drawers in the bureau, water in the pitcher by the washbasin, fresh towels on the bedstead. Downstairs in the family room* KATE *turning to a mirror hastily adjusts her bonnet, watched by a Negro servant in an apron,* VINEY.)

VINEY: Let Mr. Jimmy go by hisself, you been pokin' that garden all day, you ought to rest your feet.

KATE: I can't wait to see her, Viney.

VINEY: Maybe she ain't gone be on this train neither.

KATE: Maybe she is.

VINEY: And maybe she ain't.

KATE: And maybe she is. Where's Helen?

VINEY: She upstairs, smellin' around. She know somethin' funny's goin' on.

KATE: Let her have her supper as soon as Mildred's in bed, and tell Captain Keller when he comes that we'll be delayed tonight.

VINEY: Again.

KATE: I don't think we need say *again*. Simply delayed will do.

(*She runs upstairs to* ANNIE'S *room,* VINEY *speaking after her.*)

VINEY: I mean that's what he gone say. "What, again?"

(VINEY *works at setting the table. Upstairs* KATE *stands in the doorway, watching* HELEN'S *groping explorations.*)

KATE: Yes, we're expecting someone. Someone for my Helen.

(HELEN *happens upon her skirt, clutches her leg;* KATE *in a tired dismay kneels to tidy her hair and soiled pinafore.*)

Oh, dear, this was clean not an hour ago.

(HELEN *feels her bonnet, shakes her head darkly, and tugs to get it off.* KATE *retains it with one hand, diverts* HELEN *by opening her other hand under her nose.*)

Here. For while I'm gone.

(HELEN *sniffs, reaches, and pops something into her mouth, while* KATE *speaks a bit guiltily.*)

I don't think one peppermint drop will spoil your supper.

(*She gives* HELEN *a quick kiss, evades her hands, and hurries downstairs again. Meanwhile* CAPTAIN KELLER

*has entered the yard from around the rear of the
house, newspaper under arm, cleaning off and munch-
ing on some radishes; he sees* JAMES *lounging at the
porch post.*)

KELLER: Jimmie?

JAMES [UNMOVING]: Sir?

KELLER [EYES HIM]: You don't look dressed for anything
useful, boy.

JAMES: I'm not. It's for Miss Sullivan.

KELLER: Needn't keep holding up that porch, we have
wooden posts for that. I asked you to see that those
strawberry plants were moved this evening.

JAMES: I'm moving your—Mrs. Keller, instead. To the
station.

KELLER [HEAVILY]: Mrs. Keller. Must you always speak
of her as though you haven't met the lady?

(KATE *comes out on the porch, and* JAMES *inclines
his head.*)

JAMES [IRONIC]: Mother.

(*He starts off the porch, but sidesteps* KELLER's *glare
like a blow.*)

I said mother!

KATE: Captain.

KELLER: Evening, my dear.

KATE: We're off to meet the train, Captain. Supper will
be a trifle delayed tonight.

KELLER: What, again?

KATE [BACKING OUT]: With your permission, Captain?

(*And they are gone.* KELLER *watches them offstage,
morosely.*

Upstairs HELEN *meanwhile has groped for her mother,
touched her cheek in a meaningful gesture, waited,*

touched her cheek, waited, then found the open door, and made her way down. Now she comes into the family room, touches her cheek again; VINEY *regards her.*)

VINEY: What you want, honey, your momma?

(HELEN *touches her cheek again.* VINEY *goes to the sideboard, gets a tea-cake, gives it into* HELEN's *hand;* HELEN *pops it into her mouth.*)

Guess one little tea-cake ain't gone ruin your appetite.

(*She turns* HELEN *toward the door.* HELEN *wanders out onto the porch, as* KELLER *comes up the steps. Her hands encounter him, and she touches her cheek again, waits.*)

KELLER: She's gone.

(*He is awkward with her; when he puts his hand on her head, she pulls away.* KELLER *stands regarding her, heavily.*)

She's gone, my son and I don't get along, you don't know I'm your father, no one likes me, and supper's delayed.

(HELEN *touches her cheek, waits.* KELLER *fishes in his pocket.*)

Here. I brought you some stick candy, one nibble of sweets can't do any harm.

(*He gives her a large stick candy;* HELEN *falls to it.* VINEY *peers out the window.*)

VINEY [REPROACHFULLY]: Cap'n Keller, now how'm I

gone get her to eat her supper you fill her up with
that trash?

KELLER [ROARS]: Tend to your work!

(VINEY *beats a rapid retreat.* KELLER *thinks better of
it, and tries to get the candy away from* HELEN, *but*
HELEN *hangs on to it; and when* KELLER *pulls, she
gives his leg a kick.* KELLER *hops about,* HELEN *takes
refuge with the candy down behind the pump, and*
KELLER *then irately flings his newspaper on the porch
floor, stamps into the house past* VINEY *and disappears.*

The lights half dim on the homestead, where VINEY
and HELEN *going about their business soon find their
way off. Meanwhile, the railroad sounds off left have
mounted in a crescendo to a climax typical of a depot
at arrival time, the lights come up on stage left, and
we see a suggestion of a station. Here* ANNIE *in her
smoked glasses and disarrayed by travel is waiting
with her suitcase, while* JAMES *walks to meet her; she
has a battered paper-bound book, which is a Perkins
report, under her arm.*)

JAMES [COOLLY]: Miss Sullivan?
ANNIE [CHEERILY]: Here! At last, I've been on trains so
many days I thought they must be backing up every
time I dozed off—
JAMES: I'm James Keller.
ANNIE: James?

(*The name stops her.*)

I had a brother Jimmie. Are you Helen's?
JAMES: I'm only half a brother. You're to be her gov-
erness?
ANNIE [LIGHTLY]: Well. Try!
JAMES [EYING HER]: You look like half a governess.

(KATE *enters.* ANNIE *stands moveless, while* JAMES

takes her suitcase. KATE's *gaze on her is doubtful, troubled.*)

Mrs. Keller, Miss Sullivan.

(KATE *takes her hand.*)

KATE [SIMPLY]: We've met every train for two days.

(ANNIE *looks at* KATE's *face, and her good humor comes back.*)

ANNIE: I changed trains every time they stopped, the man who sold me that ticket ought to be tied to the tracks—
JAMES: You have a trunk, Miss Sullivan?
ANNIE: Yes.

(*She passes* JAMES *a claim check, and he bears the suitcase out behind them.* ANNIE *holds the battered book.* KATE *is studying her face, and* ANNIE *returns the gaze; this is a mutual appraisal, southern gentlewoman and working-class Irish girl, and* ANNIE *is not quite comfortable under it.*)

You didn't bring Helen, I was hoping you would.
KATE: No, she's home.

(*A pause.* ANNIE *tries to make ladylike small talk, though her energy now and then erupts; she catches herself up whenever she hears it.*)

ANNIE: You—live far from town, Mrs. Keller?
KATE: Only a mile.
ANNIE: Well. I suppose I can wait one more mile. But don't be surprised if I get out to push the horse!
KATE: Helen's waiting for you, too. There's been such a bustle in the house, she expects something, heaven knows what.

(*Now she voices part of her doubt, not as such, but* ANNIE *understands it.*)

I expected—a desiccated spinster. You're very young.

ANNIE [RESOLUTELY]: Oh, you should have seen me when I left Boston. I got much older on this trip.

KATE: I mean, to teach anyone as difficult as Helen.

ANNIE: *I* mean to try. They can't put you in jail for trying!

KATE: Is it possible, even? To teach a deaf-blind child *half* of what an ordinary child learns—has that ever been done?

ANNIE: Half?

KATE: A tenth.

ANNIE [RELUCTANTLY]: No.

(KATE'S *face loses its remaining hope, still appraising her youth.*)

Dr. Howe did wonders, but—an ordinary child? No, never. But then I thought when I was going over his reports—

(*She indicates the one in her hand*)

—he never treated them like ordinary children. More like—eggs everyone was afraid would break.

KATE [A PAUSE]: May I ask how old you are?

ANNIE: Well, I'm not in my teens, you know! I'm twenty.

KATE: All of twenty.

(ANNIE *takes the bull by the horns, valiantly.*)

ANNIE: Mrs. Keller, don't lose heart just because I'm not on my last legs. I have three big advantages over Dr. Howe that money couldn't buy for you. One is his work behind me, I've read every word he wrote about it and he wasn't exactly what you'd call a man of few words. Another is to *be* young, why, I've got energy to do anything. The third is, I've been blind.

(But it costs her something to say this.)

KATE [QUIETLY]: Advantages.

ANNIE [WRY]: Well, some have the luck of the Irish, some do not.

(KATE smiles; she likes her.)

KATE: What will you try to teach her first?

ANNIE: First, last, and—in between, language.

KATE: Language.

ANNIE: Language is to the mind more than light is to the eye. Dr. Howe said that.

KATE: Language.

(She shakes her head.)

We can't get through to teach her to sit still. You *are* young, despite your years, to have such—confidence. Do you, inside?

(ANNIE studies her face; she likes her, too.)

ANNIE: No, to tell you the truth I'm as shaky inside as a baby's rattle!

(They smile at each other, and KATE pats her hand.)

KATE: Don't be.

(JAMES returns to usher them off.)

We'll do all we can to help, and to make you feel at home. Don't think of us as strangers, Miss Annie.

ANNIE [CHEERILY]: Oh, strangers aren't so strange to me. I've known them all my life!

(KATE smiles again, ANNIE smiles back, and they precede JAMES offstage.

*The lights dim on them, having simultaneously risen
full on the house;* VINEY *has already entered the family
room, taken a water pitcher, and come out and down
to the pump. She pumps real water. As she looks offstage, we hear the clop of hoofs, a carriage stopping,
and voices.)*

VINEY: Cap'n Keller! Cap'n Keller, they comin'!

(She goes back into the house, as KELLER *comes out
on the porch to gaze.)*

She sure 'nuff came, Cap'n.

*(*KELLER *descends, and crosses toward the carriage;
this conversation begins offstage and moves on.)*

KELLER [VERY COURTLY]: Welcome to Ivy Green, Miss
Sullivan. I take it you are Miss Sullivan—
KATE: My husband, Miss Annie, Captain Keller.
ANNIE [HER BEST BEHAVIOR]: Captain, how do you do.
KELLER: A pleasure to see you, at last. I trust you had an
agreeable journey?
ANNIE: Oh, I had several! When did this country get so
big?
JAMES: Where would you like the trunk, father?
KELLER: Where Miss Sullivan can get at it, I imagine.
ANNIE: Yes, please. Where's Helen?
KELLER: In the hall, Jimmie—
KATE: We've put you in the upstairs corner room, Miss
Annie, if there's any breeze at all this summer,
you'll feel it—

(In the house the setter BELLE *flees into the family
room, pursued by* HELEN *with groping hands; the
dog doubles back out the same door, and* HELEN
*still groping for her makes her way out to the
porch; she is messy, her hair tumbled, her pinafore
now ripped, her shoelaces untied.* KELLER *acquires*

the suitcase, and ANNIE *gets her hands on it too,
though still endeavoring to live up to the general
air of propertied manners.*)

KELLER: *And* the suitcase—
ANNIE [PLEASANTLY]: I'll take the suitcase, thanks.
KELLER: Not at all, I have it, Miss Sullivan.
ANNIE: I'd like it.
KELLER [GALLANTLY]: I couldn't think of it, Miss Sul-
   livan. You'll find in the south we—
ANNIE: Let me.
KELLER: —view women as the flowers of civiliza—
ANNIE [IMPATIENTLY]: I've got something in it for Helen!

(*She tugs it free;* KELLER *stares.*)

Thank you. When do I see her?
KATE: There. There is Helen.

(ANNIE *turns, and sees* HELEN *on the porch. A
moment of silence. Then* ANNIE *begins across the
yard to her, lugging her suitcase.*)

KELLER [SOTTO VOCE]: Katie—

(KATE *silences him with a hand on his arm. When*
ANNIE *finally reaches the porch steps she stops,
contemplating* HELEN *for a last moment before entering her world. Then she drops the suitcase on
the porch with intentional heaviness,* HELEN *starts
with the jar, and comes to grope over it.* ANNIE *puts
forth her hand, and touches* HELEN'S. HELEN *at once
grasps it, and commences to explore it, like reading
a face. She moves her hand on to* ANNIE'S *forearm,
and dress; and* ANNIE *brings her face within reach of*
HELEN'S *fingers, which travel over it, quite without
timidity, until they encounter and push aside the
smoked glasses.* ANNIE'S *gaze is grave, unpitying, very
attentive. She puts her hands on* HELEN'S *arms, but*

HELEN *at once pulls away, and they confront each
other with a distance between. Then* HELEN *returns
to the suitcase, tries to open it, cannot.* ANNIE *points*
HELEN'S *hand overhead.* HELEN *pulls away, tries to
open the suitcase again;* ANNIE *points her hand over
head again.* HELEN *points overhead, a question, and*
ANNIE, *drawing* HELEN'S *hand to her own face, nods.*
HELEN *now begins tugging the suitcase toward the
door, when* ANNIE *tries to take it from her, she fights
her off and backs through the doorway with it.* ANNIE
*stands a moment, then follows her in, and together
they get the suitcase up the steps into* ANNIE'S *room.)*

KATE: Well?

KELLER: She's very rough, Katie.

KATE· I like her, Captain.

KELLER: Certainly rear a peculiar kind of young woman
in the north. How old is she?

KATE [VAGUELY]: Ohh— Well, she's not in her teens, you
know.

KELLER: She's only a child. What's her family like,
shipping her off alone this far?

KATE: I couldn't learn. She's very closemouthed about
some things.

KELLER: Why does she wear those glasses? I like to see
a person's eyes when I talk to—

KATE: For the sun. She was blind.

KELLER: Blind.

KATE: She's had nine operations on her eyes. One just
before she left.

KELLER: Blind, good heavens, do they expect one blind
child to teach another? Has she experience at least,
how long did she teach there?

KATE: She was a pupil.

KELLER [HEAVILY]: Katie, Katie. This is her first position?

KATE [BRIGHT VOICE]: She was valedictorian—

KELLER: Here's a houseful of grownups can't cope with
the child, how can an inexperienced half-blind Yankee
schoolgirl manage her?

(JAMES *moves in with the trunk on his shoulder.*)

JAMES [EASILY]: Great improvement. Now we have two
of them to look after.
KELLER: You look after those strawberry plants!

(JAMES *stops with the trunk.* KELLER *turns from him
without another word, and marches off.*)

JAMES: Nothing I say is right.
KATE: Why say anything?

(*She calls.*)

Don't be long, Captain, we'll have supper right away—

(*She goes into the house, and through the rear door
of the family room.* JAMES *trudges in with the trunk,
takes it up the steps to* ANNIE'S *room, and sets it
down outside the door. The lights elsewhere dim
somewhat.*

Meanwhile, inside, ANNIE *has given* HELEN *a key;
while* ANNIE *removes her bonnet,* HELEN *unlocks and
opens the suitcase. The first thing she pulls out is
a voluminous shawl. She fingers it until she perceives
what it is; then she wraps it around her, and acquir-
ing* ANNIE'S *bonnet and smoked glasses as well, dons
the lot: the shawl swamps her, and the bonnet settles
down upon the glasses, but she stands before a mirror
cocking her head to one side, then to the other, in a
mockery of adult action.* ANNIE *is amused, and talks
to her as one might to a kitten, with no trace of
company manners.*)

ANNIE: All the trouble I went to and that's how I look?

(HELEN *then comes back to the suitcase, gropes for
more, lifts out a pair of female drawers.*)

Oh, no. Not the drawers!

(*But* HELEN *discarding them comes to the elegant doll.
Her fingers explore its features, and when she raises
it and finds its eyes open and close, she is at first
startled, then delighted. She picks it up, taps its head
vigorously, taps her own chest, and nods questioningly.*
ANNIE *takes her finger, points it to the doll, points it
to* HELEN, *and touching it to her own face, also nods.*
HELEN *sits back on her heels, clasps the doll to herself,
and rocks it.* ANNIE *studies her, still in bonnet and
smoked glasses like a caricature of herself, and addresses her humorously.*)

All right, Miss O'Sullivan. Let's begin with doll.

(*She takes* HELEN'S *hand; in her palm* ANNIE'S *forefinger points, thumb holding her other fingers
clenched.*)

D.

(*Her thumb next holds all her fingers clenched,
touching* HELEN'S *palm.*)

O.

(*Her thumb and forefinger extend.*)

L.

(*Same contact repeated.*)

L.

(*She puts* HELEN'S *hand to the doll.*)

Doll.

JAMES: You spell pretty well.

(ANNIE *in one hurried move gets the drawers swiftly
back into the suitcase, the lid banged shut, and her
head turned, to see* JAMES *leaning in the doorway.*)

Finding out if she's ticklish? She is.

(ANNIE *regards him stonily, but* HELEN *after a scowling moment tugs at her hand again, imperious.*
ANNIE *repeats the letters, and* HELEN *interrupts her
fingers in the middle, feeling each of them, puzzled.*
ANNIE *touches* HELEN'S *hand to the doll, and begins
spelling into it again.*)

JAMES: What is it, a game?
ANNIE [CURTLY]: An alphabet.
JAMES: Alphabet?
ANNIE: For the deaf.

(HELEN *now repeats the finger movements in air,
exactly, her head cocked to her own hand, and*
ANNIE'S *eyes suddenly gleam.*)

Ho. How *bright* she is!
JAMES: You think she knows what she's doing?

(*He takes* HELEN'S *hand, to throw a meaningless
gesture into it; she repeats this one too.*)

She imitates everything, she's a monkey.
ANNIE [VERY PLEASED]: Yes, she's a bright little monkey,
all right.

(*She takes the doll from* HELEN, *and reaches for her
hand;* HELEN *instantly grabs the doll back.* ANNIE
takes it again, and HELEN'S *hand next, but* HELEN *is
incensed now; when* ANNIE *draws her hand to her face
to shake her head no, then tries to spell to her,* HELEN

slaps at ANNIE'S *face.* ANNIE *grasps* HELEN *by both
arms, and swings her into a chair, holding her pinned
there, kicking, while glasses, doll, bonnet fly in various
directions.* JAMES *laughs.*)

JAMES: She wants her doll back.

ANNIE: When she spells it.

JAMES Spell, she doesn't know the thing has a name,
even.

ANNIE: Of course not, who expects her to, now? All I
want is her fingers to learn the letters.

JAMES: Won't mean anything to her.

(ANNIE *gives him a look. She then tries to form*
HELEN'S *fingers into the letters, but* HELEN *swings a
haymaker instead, which* ANNIE *barely ducks, at once
pinning her down again.*)

Doesn't like that alphabet, Miss Sullivan. You in-
vent it yourself?

(HELEN *is now in a rage, fighting tooth and nail to
get out of the chair, and* ANNIE *answers while struggling and dodging her kicks.*)

ANNIE: Spanish monks under a—vow of silence. Which
I wish *you'd* take!

(*And suddenly releasing* HELEN'S *hands, she comes and
shuts the door in* JAMES' *face.* HELEN *drops to the
floor, groping around for the doll.* ANNIE *looks around
desperately, sees her purse on the bed, rummages in
it, and comes up with a battered piece of cake
wrapped in newspaper; with her foot she moves the
doll deftly out of the way of* HELEN'S *groping, and
going on her knee she lets* HELEN *smell the cake.
When* HELEN *grabs for it,* ANNIE *removes the cake
and spells quickly into the reaching hand.*)

Cake. From Washington up north, it's the best I can
do.

(HELEN'S *hand waits, baffled.* ANNIE *repeats it.*)

C, a, k, e. Do what my fingers do, never mind what
it means.

(*She touches the cake briefly to* HELEN'S *nose, pats
her hand, presents her own hand.* HELEN *spells the
letters rapidly back.* ANNIE *pats her hand enthusias-
tically, and gives her the cake;* HELEN *crams it into
her mouth with both hands.* ANNIE *watches her, with
humor.*)

Get it down fast, maybe I'll steal that back too. Now.

(*She takes the doll, touches it to* HELEN'S *nose, and
spells again into her hand.*)

D, o, l, l. Think it over.

(HELEN *thinks it over, while* ANNIE *presents her own
hand. Then* HELEN *spells three letters.* ANNIE *waits a
second, then completes the word for* HELEN *in her
palm.*)

L.

(*She hands over the doll, and* HELEN *gets a good grip
on its leg.*)

Imitate now, understand later. End of the first les—

(*She never finishes, because* HELEN *swings the doll
with a furious energy, it hits* ANNIE *squarely in the
face, and she falls back with a cry of pain, her
knuckles up to her mouth.* HELEN *waits, tensed for*

further combat. When ANNIE *lowers her knuckles she
looks at blood on them; she works her lips, gets to
her feet, finds the mirror, and bares her teeth at herself. Now she is furious herself.)*

You little wretch, no one's taught you *any* manners?
I'll—

(But rounding from the mirror she sees the door slam,
HELEN *and the doll are on the outside, and* HELEN *is
turning the key in the lock.* ANNIE *darts over, to pull
the knob, the door is locked fast. She yanks it again.)*

Helen! Helen, let me out of—

(She bats her brow at the folly of speaking, but
JAMES, *now downstairs, hears her and turns to see*
HELEN *with the key and doll groping her way down
the steps,* JAMES *takes in the whole situation, makes
a move to intercept* HELEN, *but then changes his
mind, lets her pass, and amusedly follows her out onto
the porch Upstairs* ANNIE *meanwhile rattles the knob,
kneels, peers through the keyhole, gets up. She goes
to the window, looks down, frowns.* JAMES *from the
yard sings gaily up to her:)*

JAMES:
    *Buffalo girl, are you coming out tonight,
    Coming out tonight,
    Coming out—*

(He drifts back into the house. ANNIE *takes a hand-
kerchief, nurses her mouth, stands in the middle of the
room, staring at door and window in turn, and so
catches sight of herself in the mirror, her cheek
scratched, her hair dishevelled, her handkerchief
bloody, her face disgusted with herself. She addresses
the mirror, with some irony.)*

ANNIE: Don't worry. They'll find you, you're not lost. Only out of place.

(*But she coughs, spits something into her palm, and stares at it, outraged.*)

And toothless.

(*She winces.*)

Oo! It hurts.

(*She pours some water into the basin, dips the hand-kerchief, and presses it to her mouth. Standing there, bent over the basin in pain—with the rest of the set dim and unreal, and the lights upon her taking on the subtle color of the past—she hears again, as do we, the faraway voices, and slowly she lifts her head to them; the boy's voice is the same, the others are cracked old crones in a nightmare, and perhaps we see their shadows.*)

BOY'S VOICE: It hurts. Annie, it hurts.
FIRST CRONE'S VOICE: Keep that brat shut up, can't you, girlie, how's a body to get any sleep in this damn ward?
BOY'S VOICE: It hurts. It hurts.
SECOND CRONE'S VOICE: Shut up, you!
BOY'S VOICE: Annie, when are we goin' home? You promised!
ANNIE: Jimmie—
BOY'S VOICE: Forever and ever, you said forever—

(ANNIE *drops the handkerchief, averts to the window, and is arrested there by the next cry.*)

Annie? Annie, you there? Annie! It *hurts!*
THIRD CRONE'S VOICE: Grab him, he's fallin'!
BOY'S VOICE: *Annie!*

DOCTOR'S VOICE [A PAUSE, SLOWLY]: Little girl. Little girl, I must tell you your brother will be going on a—

(*But* ANNIE *claps her hands to her ears, to shut this out, there is instant silence.*

As the lights bring the other areas in again, JAMES *goes to the steps to listen for any sound from upstairs.* KELLER *re-entering from left crosses toward the house; he passes* HELEN *en route to her retreat under the pump.* KATE *re-enters the rear door of the family room, with flowers for the table.*)

KATE: Supper is ready, Jimmie, will you call your father?
JAMES: Certainly.

(*But he calls up the stairs, for* ANNIE's *benefit:*)

Father! Supper!
KELLER [AT THE DOOR]: No need to shout, I've been cooling my heels for an hour. Sit down.
JAMES: Certainly.
KELLER: Viney!

(VINEY *backs in with a roast, while they get settled around the table.*)

VINEY: Yes, Cap'n, right here.
KATE: Mildred went directly to sleep, Viney?
VINEY: Oh yes, that babe's a angel.
KATE: And Helen had a good supper?
VINEY [VAGUELY]: I dunno, Miss Kate, somehow she didn't have much of a appetite tonight—
KATE [A BIT GUILTY]: Oh. Dear.
KELLER [HASTILY]: Well, now. Couldn't say the same for my part, I'm famished. Katie, your plate.
KATE [LOOKING]: But where is Miss Annie?

(*A silence.*)

JAMES [PLEASANTLY]: In her room.

KELLER: In her room? Doesn't she know hot food must be eaten hot? Go bring her down at once, Jimmie.

JAMES [RISES]: Certainly. I'll get a ladder.

KELLER [STARES]: What?

JAMES: I'll need a ladder. Shouldn't take me long.

KATE [STARES]: What shouldn't take you—

KELLER: Jimmie, do as I say! Go upstairs at once and tell Miss Sullivan supper is getting cold—

JAMES: She's locked in her room.

KELLER: Locked in her—

KATE: What on earth are you—

JAMES: Helen locked her in and made off with the key.

KATE [RISING]: And you sit here and say nothing?

JAMES: Well, everyone's been telling me not to say anything.

(*He goes serenely out and across the yard, whistling.* KELLER *thrusting up from his chair makes for the stairs.*)

KATE: Viney, look out in back for Helen. See if she has that key.

VINEY: Yes, Miss Kate.

(VINEY *goes out the rear door.*)

KELLER [CALLING DOWN]: She's out by the pump!

(KATE *goes out on the porch after* HELEN, *while* KELLER *knocks on* ANNIE'S *door, then rattles the knob, imperiously.*)

Miss Sullivan! Are you in there?

ANNIE: Oh, I'm in here, all right.

KELLER: Is there no key on your side?

ANNIE [WITH SOME ASPERITY]: Well, if there was a key in here, I wouldn't be in here. Helen took it, the only thing on my side is me.

KELLER: Miss Sullivan. I—

(*He tries, but cannot hold it back.*)

Not in the house ten minutes, I don't see *how* you managed it!

(*He stomps downstairs again, while* ANNIE *mutters to herself.*)

ANNIE. And even I'm not on my side.
KELLER [ROARING]: Viney!
VINEY [REAPPEARING]: Yes, Cap'n?
KELLER: Put that meat back in the oven!

(VINEY *bears the roast off again, while* KELLER *strides out onto the porch.* KATE *is with* HELEN *at the pump, opening her hands.*)

KATE: She has no key.
KELLER: Nonsense, she must have the key. Have you searched in her pockets?
KATE: Yes. She doesn't have it.
KELLER: Katie, she must have the key.
KATE. Would you prefer to search her yourself, Captain?
KELLER: No, I would not prefer to search her! She almost took my kneecap off this evening, when I tried merely to—

(JAMES *reappears carrying a long ladder, with* PERCY *running after him to be in on things.*)

Take that ladder back!
JAMES: Certainly.

(*He turns around with it.* MARTHA *comes skipping around the upstage corner of the house to be in on things, accompanied by the setter* BELLE.)

KATE: She could have hidden the key.

KELLER: Where?

KATE: Anywhere. Under a stone. In the flower beds. In the grass—

KELLER: Well, I can't plow up the entire grounds to find a missing key! Jimmie!

JAMES: Sir?

KELLER: Bring me a ladder!

JAMES: Certainly.

(VINEY *comes around the downstage side of the house to be in on things; she has* MILDRED *over her shoulder, bleating.* KELLER *places the ladder against* ANNIE'S *window and mounts.* ANNIE *meanwhile is running about making herself presentable, washing the blood off her mouth, straightening her clothes, tidying her hair. Another Negro servant enters to gaze in wonder, increasing the gathering ring of spectators.*)

KATE [SHARPLY]: What is Mildred doing up?

VINEY: Cap'n woke her, ma'am, all that hollerin'.

KELLER: Miss Sullivan!

(ANNIE *comes to the window, with as much air of gracious normality as she can manage;* KELLER *is at the window.*)

ANNIE [BRIGHTLY]: Yes, Captain Keller?

KELLER: Come out!

ANNIE: I don't see how I can. There isn't room.

KELLER: I intend to carry you. Climb onto my shoulder and hold tight.

ANNIE: Oh, no. It's—very chivalrous of you, but I'd really prefer to—

KELLER: Miss Sullivan, follow instructions! I will not have you also tumbling out of our windows.

(ANNIE *obeys, with some misgivings.*)

I hope this is not a sample of what we may expect from you. In the way of simplifying the work of looking after Helen.

ANNIE: Captain Keller, I'm perfectly able to go down a ladder under my own—

KELLER: I doubt it, Miss Sullivan. Simply hold onto my neck.

(He begins down with her, while the spectators stand in a wide and somewhat awe-stricken circle, watching. KELLER *half-misses a rung, and* ANNIE *grabs at his whiskers.)*

My *neck*, Miss Sullivan!

ANNIE: I'm sorry to inconvenience you this way—

KELLER: No inconvenience, other than having that door taken down and the lock replaced, if we fail to find that key.

ANNIE. Oh, I'll look everywhere for it.

KELLER: Thank you. Do not look in any rooms that can be locked. There.

(He stands her on the ground. JAMES *applauds.)*

ANNIE: Thank you very much.

(She smooths her skirt, looking as composed and ladylike as possible. KELLER *stares around at the spectators.)*

KELLER: Go, go, back to your work. What are you looking at here? There's nothing here to look at.

(They break up, move off.)

Now would it be possible for us to have supper, like other people?

(He marches into the house.)

KATE: Viney, serve supper. I'll put Mildred to sleep.

(They all go in. JAMES is the last to leave, murmuring to ANNIE with a gesture.)

JAMES: Might as well leave the l, a, d, d, e, r, hm?

(ANNIE ignores him, looking at HELEN; JAMES goes in too. Imperceptibly the lights commence to narrow down. ANNIE and HELEN are now alone in the yard, HELEN seated at the pump, where she has been oblivious to it all, a battered little savage, playing with the doll in a picture of innocent contentment. ANNIE comes near, leans against the house, and taking off her smoked glasses, studies her, not without awe. Presently HELEN rises, gropes around to see if anyone is present, ANNIE evades her hand, and when HELEN is satisfied she is alone, the key suddenly protrudes out of her mouth. She takes it in her fingers, stands thinking, gropes to the pump, lifts a loose board, drops the key into the well, and hugs herself gleefully. ANNIE stares. But after a moment she shakes her head to herself, she cannot keep the smile from her lips.)

ANNIE: You *devil*.

(Her tone is one of great respect, humor, and acceptance of challenge.)

You think I'm so easily gotten rid of? You have a thing or two to learn, first. I have nothing else to do.

(She goes up the steps to the porch, but turns for a final word, almost of warning.)

And nowhere to go.

(And presently she moves into the house to the others, as the lights dim down and out, except for the small circle upon HELEN *solitary at the pump, which ends the act.)*

ACT II

IT IS EVENING.

The only room visible in the KELLER *house is* ANNIE's, *where by lamplight* ANNIE *in a shawl is at a desk writing a letter; at her bureau* HELEN *in her customary unkempt state is tucking her doll in the bottom drawer as a cradle, the contents of which she has dumped out, creating as usual a fine disorder.*

ANNIE *mutters each word as she writes her letter, slowly, her eyes close to and almost touching the page, to follow with difficulty her penwork.*

ANNIE: ". . . and, nobody, here, has, attempted, to, control, her. The, greatest, problem, I, have, is, how, to, disipline, her, without, breaking, her, spirit."

(Resolute voice)

"But, I, shall, insist, on, reasonable, obedience, from, the, start—"

(At which point HELEN, *groping about on the desk, knocks over the inkwell.* ANNIE *jumps up, rescues her letter, rights the inkwell, grabs a towel to stem the spillage, and then wipes at* HELEN's *hands;* HELEN *as always pulls free, but not until* ANNIE *first gets three letters into her palm.)*

Ink.

*(*HELEN *is enough interested in and puzzled by this spelling that she proffers her hand again; so* ANNIE

48

spells and impassively dunks it back in the spillage.)

Ink. It has a name.

(She wipes the hand clean, and leads HELEN *to her bureau, where she looks for something to engage her. She finds a sewing card, with needle and thread, and going to her knees, shows* HELEN's *hand how to connect one row of holes.)*

Down. Under. Up. And be careful of the needle—

*(*HELEN *gets it, and* ANNIE *rises.)*

Fine. You keep out of the ink and perhaps I can keep out of—the soup.

(She returns to the desk, tidies it, and resumes writing her letter, bent close to the page.)

"These, blots, are, her, handiwork. I—"

(She is interrupted by a gasp: HELEN *has stuck her finger, and sits sucking at it, darkly. Then with vengeful resolve she seizes her doll, and is about to dash its brains out on the floor when* ANNIE *diving catches it in one hand, which she at once shakes with hopping pain but otherwise ignores, patiently.)*

All right, let's try temperance.

(Taking the doll, she kneels, goes through the motion of knocking its head on the floor, spells into HELEN's *hand:)*

Bad, girl.

(She lets HELEN *feel the grieved expression on her face.* HELEN *imitates it. Next she makes* HELEN *caress*

*the doll and kiss the hurt spot and hold it gently in
her arms, then spells into her hand:)*

Good, girl.

(She lets HELEN *feel the smile on her face.* HELEN
*sits with a scowl, which suddenly clears; she pats the
doll, kisses it, wreathes her-face in a large artificial
smile, and bears the doll to the washstand, where she
carefully sits it.* ANNIE *watches, pleased.)*

Very good girl—

(Whereupon HELEN *elevates the pitcher and dashes
it on the floor instead.* ANNIE *leaps to her feet, and
stands inarticulate;* HELEN *calmly gropes back to sit to
the sewing card and needle.*

ANNIE *manages to achieve self-control. She picks up a
fragment or two of the pitcher, sees* HELEN *is puzzling
over the card, and resolutely kneels to demonstrate it
again. She spells into* HELEN'S *hand.*

KATE *meanwhile coming around the corner with
folded sheets on her arm, halts at the doorway and
watches them for a moment in silence; she is moved,
but level.)*

KATE [PRESENTLY]: What are you saying to her?

*(*ANNIE *glancing up is a bit embarrassed, and rises
from the spelling, to find her company manners.)*

ANNIE: Oh, I was just making conversation. Saying it was
a sewing card.
KATE: But does that—

(She imitates with her fingers)

—mean that to her?

ANNIE: No. No, she won't know what spelling is till she knows what a word is.

KATE: Yet you keep spelling to her. Why?

ANNIE [CHEERILY]: I like to hear myself talk!

KATE: The Captain says it's like spelling to the fence post.

ANNIE [A PAUSE]: Does he, now.

KATE: Is it?

ANNIE: No, it's how I watch you talk to Mildred.

KATE: Mildred.

ANNIE: Any baby. Gibberish, grown-up gibberish, baby-talk gibberish, do they understand one word of it to start? Somehow they begin to. If they hear it, I'm letting Helen hear it.

KATE: Other children are not—impaired.

ANNIE: Ho, there's nothing impaired in that head, it works like a mousetrap!

KATE [SMILES]: But after a child hears how many words, Miss Annie, a million?

ANNIE: I guess no mother's ever minded enough to count.

(She drops her eyes to spell into HELEN's hand, again indicating the card; HELEN spells back, and ANNIE is amused.)

KATE [TOO QUICKLY]: What did she spell?

ANNIE: I spelt card. She spelt cake!

(She takes in KATE's quickness, and shakes her head, gently.)

No, it's only a finger-game to her, Mrs. Keller. What she has to learn first is that things have names.

KATE: And when will she learn?

ANNIE: Maybe after a million and one words.

(They hold each other's gaze; KATE then speaks quietly.)

KATE: I should like to learn those letters, Miss Annie.

ANNIE [PLEASED]: I'll teach you tomorrow morning. That makes only half a million each!

KATE [THEN]: It's her bedtime.

(ANNIE *reaches for the sewing card,* HELEN *objects,* ANNIE *insists, and* HELEN *gets rid of* ANNIE'S *hand by jabbing it with the needle.* ANNIE *gasps, and moves to grip* HELEN'S *wrist; but* KATE *intervenes with a proffered sweet, and* HELEN *drops the card, crams the sweet into her mouth, and scrambles up to search her mother's hands for more.* ANNIE *nurses her wound, staring after the sweet.*)

I'm sorry, Miss Annie.

ANNIE [INDIGNANTLY]: Why does she get a reward? For stabbing me?

KATE: Well—

(*Then, tiredly*)

We catch our flies with honey, I'm afraid. We haven't the heart for much else, and so many times she simply cannot be compelled.

ANNIE [OMINOUS]: Yes. I'm the same way myself.

(KATE *smiles, and leads* HELEN *off around the corner.* ANNIE *alone in her room picks up things and in the act of removing* HELEN'S *doll gives way to unmannerly temptation: she throttles it. She drops it on her bed, and stands pondering. Then she turns back, sits decisively, and writes again, as the lights dim on her.*)

(*Grimly*)

"The, more, I, think, the, more, certain, I, am, that, obedience, is, the, gateway, through, which, knowledge, enters, the, mind, of, the, child—"

(On the word "obedience" a shaft of sunlight hits the water pump outside, while ANNIE'S voice ends in the dark, followed by a distant cockcrow; daylight comes up over another corner of the sky, with VINEY'S voice heard at once.)

VINEY: Breakfast ready!

(VINEY comes down into the sunlight beam, and pumps a pitcherful of water. While the pitcher is brimming we hear conversation from the dark; the light grows to the family room of the house where all are either entering or already seated at breakfast, with KELLER and JAMES arguing the war. HELEN is wandering around the table to explore the contents of the other plates. When ANNIE is in her chair, she watches HELEN. VINEY re-enters, sets the pitcher on the table; KATE lifts the almost empty biscuit plate with an inquiring look, VINEY nods and bears it off back, neither of them interrupting the men. ANNIE meanwhile sits with fork quiet, watching HELEN, who at her mother's plate pokes her hand among some scrambled eggs. KATE catches ANNIE'S eyes on her, smiles with a wry gesture. HELEN moves on to JAMES's plate, the male talk continuing, JAMES deferential and KELLER overriding.)

JAMES: —no, but shouldn't we give the devil his due, father? The fact is we lost the South two years earlier when he outthought us behind Vicksburg.

KELLER: Outthought is a peculiar word for a butcher.

JAMES: Harness maker, wasn't he?

KELLER: I said butcher, his only virtue as a soldier was numbers and he led them to slaughter with no more regard than for so many sheep.

JAMES: But even if in that sense he was a butcher, the fact is he—

KELLER: And a drunken one, half the war.

JAMES: Agreed, father. If his own people said he was I can't argue he—

KELLER: Well, what is it you find to admire in such a man, Jimmie, the butchery or the drunkenness?

JAMES: Neither, father, only the fact that he beat us.

KELLER: He didn't.

JAMES: Is it your contention we won the war, sir?

KELLER: He didn't beat us at Vicksburg. We lost Vicksburg because Pemberton gave Bragg five thousand of his cavalry and Loring, whom I knew personally for a nincompoop before you were born, marched away from Champion's Hill with enough men to have held them, we lost Vicksburg by stupidity verging on treason.

JAMES: I would have said we lost Vicksburg because Grant was one thing no Yankee general was before him—

KELLER: Drunk? I doubt it.

JAMES: Obstinate.

KELLER: Obstinate. Could any of them compare even in that with old Stonewall? If he'd been there we would still have Vicksburg.

JAMES: Well, the butcher simply wouldn't give up, he tried four ways of getting around Vicksburg and on the fifth try he got around. Anyone else would have pulled north and—

KELLER: He wouldn't have got around if we'd had a Southerner in command, instead of a half-breed Yankee traitor like Pemberton—

(*While this background talk is in progress,* HELEN *is working around the table, ultimately toward* ANNIE's *plate. She messes with her hands in* JAMES's *plate, then in* KELLER's, *both men taking it so for granted they hardly notice. Then* HELEN *comes groping with soiled hands past her own plate, to* ANNIE's; *her hand goes to it, and* ANNIE, *who has been waiting, deliberately lifts and removes her hand.* HELEN *gropes again,* ANNIE *firmly pins her by the wrist, and removes her hand from the table.* HELEN *thrusts her hands again,* ANNIE *catches them, and* HELEN *begins to flail and make noises; the interruption brings* KELLER's *gaze upon them.*)

What's the matter there?

KATE: Miss Annie. You see, she's accustomed to helping herself from our plates to anything she—

ANNIE [EVENLY]: Yes, but *I'm* not accustomed to it.

KELLER: No, of course not. Viney!

KATE: Give her something, Jimmie, to quiet her.

JAMES [BLANDLY]: But her table manners are the best she has. Well.

(*He pokes across with a chunk of bacon at* HELEN's *hand, which* ANNIE *releases; but* HELEN *knocks the bacon away and stubbornly thrusts at* ANNIE's *plate,* ANNIE *grips her wrists again, the struggle mounts.*)

KELLER: Let her this time, Miss Sullivan, it's the only way we get any adult conversation. If my son's half merits that description.

(*He rises.*)

I'll get you another plate.

ANNIE [GRIPPING HELEN]: I have a plate, thank you.

KATE [CALLING]: Viney! I'm afraid what Captain Keller says is only too true, she'll persist in this until she gets her own way.

KELLER [AT THE DOOR]: Viney, bring Miss Sullivan another plate—

ANNIE [STONILY]: I have a plate, nothing's wrong with the *plate,* I intend to keep it.

(*Silence for a moment, except for* HELEN's *noises as she struggles to get loose; the* KELLERs *are a bit non-plussed, and* ANNIE *is too darkly intent on* HELEN's *manners to have any thoughts now of her own.*)

JAMES: Ha. You see why they took Vicksburg?

KELLER [UNCERTAINLY]: Miss Sullivan. One plate or another is hardly a matter to struggle with a deprived child about.

ANNIE: Oh, I'd sooner have a more—

(HELEN *begins to kick,* ANNIE *moves her ankles to the opposite side of the chair.*)

—heroic issue myself, I—

KELLER: No, I really must insist you—

(HELEN *bangs her toe on the chair and sinks to the floor, crying with rage and feigned injury;* ANNIE *keeps hold of her wrists, gazing down, while* KATE *rises.*)

Now she's hurt herself.

ANNIE [GRIMLY]: No, she hasn't.

KELLER: Will you please let her hands go?

KATE: Miss Annie, you don't know the child well enough yet, she'll keep—

ANNIE: I know an ordinary tantrum well enough, when I see one, and a badly spoiled child—

JAMES: Hear, hear.

KELLER [VERY ANNOYED]: Miss Sullivan! You would have more understanding of your pupil if you had some pity in you. Now kindly do as I—

ANNIE: Pity?

(*She releases* HELEN *to turn equally annoyed on* KELLER *across the table; instantly* HELEN *scrambles up and dives at* ANNIE's *plate. This time* ANNIE *intercepts her by pouncing on her wrists like a hawk, and her temper boils.*)

For this *tyrant?* The whole house turns on her whims, is there anything she wants she doesn't get? I'll tell

you what I pity, that the sun won't rise and set for
her all her life, and every day you're telling her it
will, what good will your pity do her when you're
under the strawberries, Captain Keller?

KELLER [OUTRAGED]: Kate, for the love of heaven will
you—

KATE: Miss Annie, please, I don't think it serves to lose
our—

ANNIE: It does you good, that's all. It's less trouble to feel
sorry for her than to teach her anything better, isn't it?

KELLER: I fail to see where you have taught her anything
yet, Miss Sullivan!

ANNIE: I'll begin this minute, if you'll leave the room,
Captain Keller!

KELLER [ASTONISHED]: Leave the—

ANNIE: Everyone, please.

(*She struggles with* HELEN, *while* KELLER *endeavors
to control his voice.*)

KELLER: Miss Sullivan, you are here only as a paid teacher.
Nothing more, and not to lecture—

ANNIE: I can't unteach her six years of pity if you can't
stand up to one tantrum! Old Stonewall, indeed. Mrs.
Keller, you promised me help.

KATE: Indeed I did, we truly want to—

ANNIE: Then leave me alone with her. Now!

KELLER [IN A WRATH]: Katie, will you come outside with
me? At once, please.

(*He marches to the front door.* KATE *and* JAMES *follow
him. Simultaneously* ANNIE *releases* HELEN'S *wrists,
and the child again sinks to the floor, kicking and
crying her weird noises;* ANNIE *steps over her to meet*
VINEY *coming in the rear doorway with biscuits and a
clean plate, surprised at the general commotion.*)

VINEY: Heaven sakes—

ANNIE: Out, please.

(*She backs* VINEY *out with one hand, closes the door on her astonished mouth, locks it, and removes the key.* KELLER *meanwhile snatches his hat from a rack, and* KATE *follows him down the porch steps.* JAMES *lingers in the doorway to address* ANNIE *across the room with a bow.*)

JAMES: If it takes all summer, general.

(ANNIE *comes over to his door in turn, removing her glasses grimly; as* KELLER *outside begins speaking,* ANNIE *closes the door on* JAMES, *locks it, removes the key, and turns with her back against the door to stare ominously at* HELEN, *kicking on the floor.*

JAMES *takes his hat from the rack, and going down the porch steps joins* KATE *and* KELLER *talking in the yard,* KELLER *in a sputter of ire.*)

KELLER: This girl, this—cub of a girl—*presumes!* I tell you, I'm of half a mind to ship her back to Boston before the week is out. You can inform her so from me!

KATE [EYEBROWS UP]: I, Captain?

KELLER: She's a *hireling!* Now I want it clear, unless there's an apology and complete change of manner she goes back on the next train! Will you make that quite clear?

KATE: Where will you be, Captain, while I am making it quite—

KELLER: At the office!

(*He begins off left, finds his napkin still in his irate hand, is uncertain with it, dabs his lips with dignity, gets rid of it in a toss to* JAMES, *and marches off.* JAMES *turns to eye* KATE.)

JAMES: Will you?

(KATE'S *mouth is set, and* JAMES *studies it lightly.*)

I thought what she said was exceptionally intelligent. I've been saying it for years.

KATE [NOT WITHOUT SCORN]: To his face?

(*She comes to relieve him of the white napkin, but reverts again with it.*)

Or will you take it, Jimmie? As a flag?

(JAMES *stalks out, much offended, and* KATE *turning stares across the yard at the house; the lights narrowing down to the following pantomime in the family room leave her motionless in the dark.*

ANNIE *meanwhile has begun by slapping both keys down on a shelf out of* HELEN'S *reach; she returns to the table, upstage.* HELEN'S *kicking has subsided, and when from the floor her hand finds* ANNIE'S *chair empty she pauses.* ANNIE *clears the table of* KATE'S, JAMES'S, *and* KELLER'S *plates; she gets back to her own across the table just in time to slide it deftly away from* HELEN'S *pouncing hand. She lifts the hand and moves it to* HELEN'S *plate, and after an instant's exploration,* HELEN *sits again on the floor and drums her heels.* ANNIE *comes around the table and resumes her chair. When* HELEN *feels her skirt again, she ceases kicking, waits for whatever is to come, renews some kicking, waits again.* ANNIE *retrieving her plate takes up a forkful of food, stops it halfway to her mouth, gazes at it devoid of appetite, and half-lowers it; but after a look at* HELEN *she sighs, dips the forkful toward* HELEN *in a for-your-sake toast, and puts it in her own mouth to chew, not without an effort.*

HELEN *now gets hold of the chair leg, and half-succeeds in pulling the chair out from under her.* ANNIE *bangs it down with her rear, heavily, and sits with all her weight.* HELEN's *next attempt to topple it is unavailing, so her fingers dive in a pinch at* ANNIE's *flank.* ANNIE *in the middle of her mouthful almost loses it with startle, and she slaps down her fork to round on* HELEN. *The child comes up with curiosity to feel what* ANNIE *is doing, so* ANNIE *resumes eating, letting* HELEN's *hand follow the movement of her fork to her mouth; whereupon* HELEN *at once reaches into* ANNIE's *plate.* ANNIE *firmly removes her hand to her own plate.* HELEN *in reply pinches* ANNIE's *thigh, a good mean pinchful that makes* ANNIE *jump.* ANNIE *sets the fork down, and sits with her mouth tight.* HELEN *digs another pinch into her thigh, and this time* ANNIE *slaps her hand smartly away;* HELEN *retaliates with a roundhouse fist that catches* ANNIE *on the ear, and* ANNIE's *hand leaps at once in a forceful slap across* HELEN's *cheek;* HELEN *is the startled one now.* ANNIE's *hand in compunction falters to her own face, but when* HELEN *hits at her again,* ANNIE *deliberately slaps her again.* HELEN *lifts her fist irresolute for another roundhouse,* ANNIE *lifts her hand resolute for another slap, and they freeze in this posture, while* HELEN *mulls it over. She thinks better of it, drops her fist, and giving* ANNIE *a wide berth, gropes around to her* MOTHER's *chair, to find it empty; she blunders her way along the table upstage, and encountering the empty chairs and missing plates, she looks bewildered; she gropes back to her* MOTHER's *chair, again touches her cheek and indicates the chair, and waits for the world to answer.*

ANNIE *now reaches over to spell into her hand, but* HELEN *yanks it away; she gropes to the front door, tries the knob, and finds the door locked, with no key. She gropes to the rear door, and finds it locked, with no key. She commences to bang on it.* ANNIE *rises, crosses, takes her wrists, draws her resisting back to the table, seats her, and releases her hands upon her plate; as* ANNIE *herself begins to sit,* HELEN

*writhes out of her chair, runs to the front door, and
tugs and kicks at it.* ANNIE *rises again, crosses, draws
her by one wrist back to the table, seats her, and
sits;* HELEN *escapes back to the door, knocking over
her* MOTHER'S *chair en route.* ANNIE *rises again in
pursuit, and this time lifts* HELEN *bodily from behind
and bears her kicking to her chair. She deposits her,
and once more turns to sit.* HELEN *scrambles out, but
as she passes* ANNIE *catches her up again from behind
and deposits her in the chair;* HELEN *scrambles out
on the other side, for the rear door, but* ANNIE *at her
heels catches her up and deposits her again in the
chair. She stands behind it.* HELEN *scrambles out to
her right, and the instant her feet hit the floor* ANNIE
*lifts and deposits her back; she scrambles out to her
left, and is at once lifted and deposited back. She tries
right again and is deposited back, and tries left again
and is deposited back, and now feints* ANNIE *to the
right but is off to her left, and is promptly deposited
back. She sits a moment, and then starts straight over
the tabletop, dishware notwithstanding;* ANNIE *hauls
her in and deposits her back, with her plate spilling
in her lap, and she melts to the floor and crawls under
the table, laborious among its legs and chairs; but*
ANNIE *is swift around the table and waiting on the
other side when she surfaces, immediately bearing her
aloft;* HELEN *clutches at* JAMES'S *chair for anchorage,
but it comes with her, and halfway back she abandons
it to the floor.* ANNIE *deposits her in her chair, and
waits.* HELEN *sits tensed motionless. Then she tenta-
tively puts out her left foot and hand,* ANNIE *inter-
poses her own hand, and at the contact* HELEN *jerks
hers in. She tries her right foot,* ANNIE *blocks it with
her own, and* HELEN *jerks hers in. Finally, leaning
back, she slumps down in her chair, in a sullen biding.*

ANNIE *backs off a step, and watches;* HELEN *offers
no move.* ANNIE *takes a deep breath. Both of them
and the room are in considerable disorder, two chairs*

down and the table a mess, but ANNIE *makes no effort
to tidy it; she only sits on her own chair, and lets her
energy refill. Then she takes up knife and fork, and
resolutely addresses her food.* HELEN's *hand comes out
to explore, and seeing it* ANNIE *sits without moving,
the child's hand goes over her hand and fork, pauses—*
ANNIE *still does not move—and withdraws. Presently
it moves for her own plate, slaps about for it, and
stops, thwarted. At this,* ANNIE *again rises, recovers*
HELEN's *plate from the floor and a handful of scattered
food from the deranged tablecloth, drops it on the
plate, and pushes the plate into contact with* HELEN's
*fist. Neither of them now moves for a pregnant mo-
ment—until* HELEN *suddenly takes a grab of food and
wolfs it down.* ANNIE *permits herself the humor of a
minor bow and warming of her hands together; she
wanders off a step or two, watching.* HELEN *cleans up
the plate.*

*After a glower of indecision, she holds the empty
plate out for more.* ANNIE *accepts it, and crossing to
the removed plates, spoons food from them onto it;
she stands debating the spoon, tapping it a few times
on* HELEN's *plate; and when she returns with the plate
she brings the spoon, too. She puts the spoon first into*
HELEN's *hand, then sets the plate down.* HELEN *discarding the spoon reaches with her hand, and* ANNIE
stops it by the wrist; she replaces the spoon in it.
HELEN *impatiently discards it again, and again* ANNIE
stops her hand, to replace the spoon in it. This time
HELEN *throws the spoon on the floor.* ANNIE *after con-
sidering it lifts* HELEN *bodily out of the chair, and in a
wrestling match on the floor closes her fingers upon the
spoon, and returns her with it to the chair.* HELEN
again throws the spoon on the floor. ANNIE *lifts her out
of the chair again; but in the struggle over the spoon*
HELEN *with* ANNIE *on her back sends her sliding over
her head;* HELEN *flees back to her chair and scrambles
into it. When* ANNIE *comes after her she clutches it for*

dear life; ANNIE *pries one hand loose, then the other, then the first again, then the other again, and then lifts* HELEN *by the waist, chair and all, and shakes the chair loose.* HELEN *wrestles to get free, but* ANNIE *pins her to the floor, closes her fingers upon the spoon, and lifts her kicking under one arm; with her other hand she gets the chair in place again, and plunks* HELEN *back on it. When she releases her hand,* HELEN *throws the spoon at her.*

ANNIE *now removes the plate of food.* HELEN *grabbing finds it missing, and commences to bang with her fists on the table.* ANNIE *collects a fistful of spoons and descends with them and the plate on* HELEN; *she lets her smell the plate, at which* HELEN *ceases banging, and* ANNIE *puts the plate down and a spoon in* HELEN's *hand.* HELEN *throws it on the floor.* ANNIE *puts another spoon in her hand.* HELEN *throws it on the floor.* ANNIE *puts another spoon in her hand.* HELEN *throws it on the floor. When* ANNIE *comes to her last spoon she sits next to* HELEN, *and gripping the spoon in* HELEN's *hand compels her to take food in it up to her mouth.* HELEN *sits with lips shut.* ANNIE *waits a stolid moment, then lowers* HELEN's *hand. She tries again;* HELEN's *lips remain shut.* ANNIE *waits, lowers* HELEN's *hand. She tries again; this time* HELEN *suddenly opens her mouth and accepts the food.* ANNIE *lowers the spoon with a sigh of relief, and* HELEN *spews the mouthful out at her face.* ANNIE *sits a moment with eyes closed, then takes the pitcher and dashes its water into* HELEN's *face, who gasps astonished.* ANNIE *with* HELEN's *hand takes up another spoonful, and shoves it into her open mouth.* HELEN *swallows involuntarily, and while she is catching her breath* ANNIE *forces her palm open, throws four swift letters into it, then another four, and bows toward her with devastating pleasantness.)*

ANNIE: Good girl.

(ANNIE *lifts* HELEN'S *hand to feel her face nodding;* HELEN *grabs a fistful of her hair, and yanks. The pain brings* ANNIE *to her knees, and* HELEN *pummels her; they roll under the table, and the lights commence to dim out on them.*

Simultaneously the light at left has been rising, slowly, so slowly that it seems at first we only imagine what is intimated in the yard: a few ghostlike figures, in silence, motionless, waiting. Now the distant belfry chimes commence to toll the hour, also very slowly, almost—it is twelve—interminably; the sense is that of a long time passing. We can identify the figures before the twelfth stroke, all facing the house in a kind of watch: KATE *is standing exactly as before, but now with the baby* MILDRED *sleeping in her arms, and placed here and there, unmoving, are* AUNT EV *in her hat with a hanky to her nose, and the two Negro children,* PERCY *and* MARTHA *with necks outstretched eagerly, and* VINEY *with a knotted kerchief on her head and a feather duster in her hand.*

The chimes cease, and there is silence. For a long moment none of the group moves.)

VINEY [PRESENTLY]: What am I gone do, Miss Kate? It's noontime, dinner's comin', I didn't get them breakfast dishes out of there yet.

(KATE *says nothing, stares at the house.* MARTHA *shifts* HELEN'S *doll in her clutch, and it plaintively says momma.*)

KATE [PRESENTLY]: You run along, Martha.

(AUNT EV *blows her nose.*)

AUNT EV [WRETCHEDLY]: I can't wait out here a minute

longer, Kate, why, this could go on all afternoon, too.
KATE: I'll tell the captain you called.
VINEY [TO THE CHILDREN]: You hear what Miss Kate say?
Never you mind what's going on here.

(Still no one moves.)

You run along tend your own bizness.

(Finally VINEY *turns on the children with the feather
duster.)*

Shoo!

*(The two children divide before her. She chases
them off.* AUNT EV *comes to* KATE, *on her dignity.)*

AUNT EV: Say what you like, Kate, but that child is a
Keller.

(She opens her parasol, preparatory to leaving.)

I needn't remind you that all the Kellers are cousins
to General Robert E. Lee. I don't know *who* that
girl is.

(She waits; but KATE *staring at the house is without
response.)*

The only Sullivan I've heard of—from Boston too, and
I'd think twice before locking her up with that kind—
is that man John L.

(And AUNT EV *departs, with head high. Presently
VINEY comes to* KATE, *her arms out for the baby.)*

VINEY: You give me her, Miss Kate, I'll sneak her in back,
to her crib.

(*But* KATE *is moveless, until* VINEY *starts to take the baby;* KATE *looks down at her before relinquishing her.*)

KATE [SLOWLY]: This child never gives me a minute's worry.

VINEY: Oh yes, this one's the angel of the family, no question bout *that*.

(*She begins off rear with the baby, heading around the house; and* KATE *now turns her back on it, her hand to her eyes. At this moment there is the slamming of a door, and when* KATE *wheels* HELEN *is blundering down the porch steps into the light, like a ruined bat out of hell.* VINEY *halts, and* KATE *runs in;* HELEN *collides with her mother's knees, and reels off and back to clutch them as her savior.* ANNIE *with smoked glasses in hand stands on the porch, also much undone, looking as though she had indeed just taken Vicksburg.* KATE *taking in* HELEN's *ravaged state becomes steely in her gaze up at* ANNIE.)

KATE: What happened?

(ANNIE *meets* KATE's *gaze, and gives a factual report, too exhausted for anything but a flat voice.*)

ANNIE: She ate from her own plate.

(*She thinks a moment.*)

She ate with a spoon. Herself.

(KATE *frowns, uncertain with thought, and glances down at* HELEN.)

And she folded her napkin.

(KATE'S *gaze now wavers, from* HELEN *to* ANNIE, *and back.*)

KATE [SOFTLY]: Folded—her napkin?

ANNIE: The room's a wreck, but her napkin is folded.

(*She pauses, then:*)

I'll be in my room, Mrs. Keller.

(*She moves to re-enter the house; but she stops at* VINEY'S *voice.*)

VINEY [CHEERY]: Don't be long, Miss Annie. Dinner be ready right away!

(VINEY *carries* MILDRED *around the back of the house.* ANNIE *stands unmoving, takes a deep breath, stares over her shoulder at* KATE *and* HELEN, *then inclines her head graciously, and goes with a slight stagger into the house. The lights in her room above steal up in readiness for her.*

KATE *remains alone with* HELEN *in the yard, standing protectively over her, in a kind of wonder.*)

KATE [SLOWLY]: Folded her napkin.

(*She contemplates the wild head in her thighs, and moves her fingertips over it, with such a tenderness, and something like a fear of its strangeness, that her own eyes close; she whispers, bending to it:*)

My Helen—folded her napkin—

(*And still erect, with only her head in surrender,* KATE *for the first time that we see loses her protracted war with grief; but she will not let a sound escape her, only the grimace of tears comes, and sobs that shake her in a grip of silence. But* HELEN *feels them, and her hand comes up in its own wondering, to interrogate her mother's face, until* KATE *buries her lips in the child's palm.*

Upstairs, ANNIE *enters her room, closes the door, and stands back against it; the lights, growing on her with their special color, commence to fade on* KATE *and* HELEN. *Then* ANNIE *goes wearily to her suitcase, and lifts it to take it toward the bed. But it knocks an object to the floor, and she turns back to regard it. A new voice comes in a cultured murmur, hesitant as with the effort of remembering a text:)*

MAN'S VOICE: This—soul—

(ANNIE *puts the suitcase down, and kneels to the object: it is the battered Perkins report, and she stands with it in her hand, letting memory try to speak:)*

This—blind, deaf, mute—woman—

(ANNIE *sits on her bed, opens the book, and finding the passage, brings it up an inch from her eyes to read, her face and lips following the overheard words, the voice quite factual now:)*

Can nothing be done to disinter this human soul? The whole neighborhood would rush to save this woman if she were buried alive by the caving in of a pit, and labor with zeal until she were dug out. Now if there were one who had as much patience as zeal, he might awaken her to a consciousness of her immortal—

(*When the boy's voice comes,* ANNIE *closes her eyes, in pain.*)

BOY'S VOICE: Annie? Annie, you there?

ANNIE: Hush.
BOY'S VOICE: Annie, what's that noise?

(ANNIE *tries not to answer; her own voice is drawn
out of her, unwilling.*)

ANNIE: Just a cot, Jimmie.
BOY'S VOICE: Where they pushin' it?
ANNIE: To the deadhouse.
BOY'S VOICE: Annie. Does it hurt, to be dead?

(ANNIE *escapes by opening her eyes, her hand works
restlessly over her cheek; she retreats into the book
again, but the cracked old crones interrupt, whispering.* ANNIE *slowly lowers the book.*)

FIRST CRONE'S VOICE: There is schools.
SECOND CRONE'S VOICE: There is schools outside—
THIRD CRONE'S VOICE: —schools where they teach blind
    ones, worse'n you—
FIRST CRONE'S VOICE: To read—
SECOND CRONE'S VOICE: To read and write—
THIRD CRONE'S VOICE: There is schools outside where
    they—
FIRST CRONE'S VOICE: There is schools—

(*Silence.* ANNIE *sits with her eyes shining, her hand
almost in a caress over the book. Then:*)

BOY'S VOICE: You ain't goin' to school, are you, Annie?
ANNIE [WHISPERING]: When I grow up.
BOY'S VOICE: You ain't either, Annie. You're goin' to stay
    here take care of me.
ANNIE: I'm goin' to school when I grow up.
BOY'S VOICE: You said we'll be together, forever and
    ever and ever—
ANNIE [FIERCE]: I'm goin' to school when I grow up!
DOCTOR'S VOICE [SLOWLY]: Little girl. Little girl, I must

tell you. Your brother will be going on a journey, soon.

(ANNIE *sits rigid, in silence. Then the boy's voice pierces it, a shriek of terror.*)

BOY'S VOICE: *Annie!*

(*It goes into* ANNIE *like a sword, she doubles onto it; the book falls to the floor. It takes her a racked moment to find herself and what she was engaged in here; when she sees the suitcase she remembers, and lifts it once again toward the bed. But the voices are with her, as she halts with suitcase in hand.*)

FIRST CRONE'S VOICE: Goodbye, Annie.
DOCTOR'S VOICE: Write me when you learn how.
SECOND CRONE'S VOICE: Don't tell anyone you came from here. Don't tell anyone—
THIRD CRONE'S VOICE: Yeah, don't tell anyone you came from—
FIRST CRONE'S VOICE: Yeah, don't tell anyone—
SECOND CRONE'S VOICE: Don't tell any—

(*The echoing voices fade. After a moment* ANNIE *lays the suitcase on the bed; and the last voice comes faintly, from far away.*)

BOY'S VOICE: Annie. It hurts, to be dead. Forever.

(ANNIE *falls to her knees by the bed, stifling her mouth in it. When at last she rolls blindly away from it, her palm comes down on the open report; she opens her eyes, regards it dully, and then, still on her knees, takes in the print.*)

MAN'S VOICE [FACTUAL]: —might awaken her to a consciousness of her immortal nature. The chance is small indeed; but with a smaller chance they would have dug desperately for her in the pit; and is the life of the soul of less import than that of the body?

(ANNIE *gets to her feet. She drops the book on the bed, and pauses over her suitcase; after a moment she unclasps and opens it. Standing before it, she comes to her decision; she at once turns to the bureau, and taking her things out of its drawers, commences to throw them into the open suitcase.*

In the darkness down left a hand strikes a match, and lights a hanging oil lamp. It is KELLER'S *hand, and his voice accompanies it, very angry; the lights rising here before they fade on* ANNIE *show* KELLER *and* KATE *inside a suggestion of a garden house, with a bay-window seat towards center and a door at back.*)

KELLER: Katie, I will not *have* it! Now you did not see when that girl after supper tonight went to look for Helen in her room—

KATE: No.

KELLER: The child practically climbed out of her window to escape from her! What kind of teacher *is* she? I thought I had seen her at her worst this morning, shouting at me, but I come home to find the entire house disorganized by her—Helen won't stay one second in the same room, won't come to the table with her, won't let herself be bathed or undressed or put to bed by her, or even by Viney now, and the end result is that *you* have to do more for the child than before we hired this girl's services! From the moment she stepped off the train she's been nothing but a burden, incompetent, impertinent, ineffectual, immodest—

KATE: She folded her napkin, Captain.

KELLER: What?

KATE: Not ineffectual. Helen did fold her napkin.

KELLER: What in heaven's name is so extraordinary about folding a napkin?

KATE [WITH SOME HUMOR]: Well. It's more than you did, Captain.

KELLER: Katie. I did not bring you all the way out here to the garden house to be frivolous. Now, how does Miss Sullivan propose to teach a deaf-blind pupil who won't let her even touch her?

KATE [A PAUSE]: I don't know.

KELLER: The fact is, today she scuttled any chance she ever had of getting along with the child. If you can see any point or purpose to her staying on here longer, it's more than—

KATE: What do you wish me to do?

KELLER: I want you to give her notice.

KATE: I can't.

KELLER: Then if you won't, I must. I simply will not—

(He is interrupted by a knock at the back door KELLER after a glance at KATE moves to open the door; ANNIE in her smoked glasses is standing outside. KELLER contemplates her, heavily.)

Miss Sullivan.

ANNIE: Captain Keller.

(She is nervous, keyed up to seizing the bull by the horns again, and she assumes a cheeriness which is not unshaky.)

Viney said I'd find you both over here in the garden house. I thought we should—have a talk?

KELLER [RELUCTANTLY]: Yes, I— Well, come in.

(ANNIE enters, and is interested in this room; she rounds on her heel, anxiously, studying it. KELLER turns the matter over to KATE, sotto voce.)

Katie

KATE [TURNING IT BACK, COURTEOUSLY]: Captain.

(KELLER *clears his throat, makes ready.*)

KELLER: I, ah—wanted first to make my position clear to
Mrs Keller, in private. I have decided I—am not
satisfied—in fact, am deeply dissatisfied—with the
manner in which—

ANNIE [INTENT]: Excuse me, is this little house ever in
use?

KELLER [WITH PATIENCE]: In the hunting season. If you
will give me your attention, Miss Sullivan.

(ANNIE *turns her smoked glasses upon him; they hold
his unwilling stare.*)

I have tried to make allowances for you because you
come from a part of the country where people are—
women, I should say—come from who—well, for
whom—

(*It begins to elude him.*)

—allowances must—be made. I have decided, never-
theless, to—that is, decided I—

(*Vexedly*)

Miss Sullivan, I find it difficult to talk through those
glasses.

ANNIE [EAGERLY, REMOVING THEM]: Oh, of course.

KELLER [DOURLY]: Why do you wear them, the sun has
been down for an hour.

ANNIE [PLEASANTLY, AT THE LAMP]: Any kind of light
hurts my eyes.

(*A silence;* KELLER *ponders her, heavily.*)

KELLER: Put them on. Miss Sullivan, I have decided to
   —give you another chance.

ANNIE [CHEERFULLY]: To do what?

KELLER: To—remain in our employ.

(ANNIE'S *eyes widen.*)

But on two conditions. I am not accustomed to
rudeness in servants or women, and that is the
first. If you are to stay, there must be a radical
change of manner.

ANNIE [A PAUSE]: Whose?

KELLER [EXPLODING]: Yours, young lady, isn't it ob-
vious? And the second is that you persuade me
there's the slightest hope of your teaching a child
who flees from you now like the plague, to anyone
else she can find in this house.

ANNIE [A PAUSE]: There isn't.

(KATE *stops sewing, and fixes her eyes upon* ANNIE.)

KATE: What, Miss Annie?

ANNIE: It's hopeless here. I can't teach a child who
runs away.

KELLER [NONPLUSSED]: Then—do I understand you—
propose—

ANNIE: Well, if we all agree it's hopeless, the next question is what—

KATE: Miss Annie.

(She is *leaning toward* ANNIE, *in deadly earnest; it
commands both* ANNIE *and* KELLER.)

I am not agreed. I think perhaps you—underesti-
mate Helen.

ANNIE: I think everybody else here does.

KATE: She did fold her napkin. She learns, she learns, do
you know she began talking when she was six months
old? She could say "water." Not really—"wahwah."

"Wahwah," but she meant water, she knew what it
meant, and only six months old, I never saw a child
so—bright, or outgoing—

(*Her voice is unsteady, but she gets it level.*)

It's still in her, somewhere, isn't it? You should have
seen her before her illness, such a good-tempered
child—

ANNIE [AGREEABLY]: She's changed.

(*A pause,* KATE *not letting her eyes go; her appeal at
last is unconditional, and very quiet.*)

KATE: Miss Annie, put up with it. And with us.
KELLER: Us!
KATE: Please? Like the lost lamb in the parable, I love
her all the more.
ANNIE: Mrs. Keller, I don't think Helen's worst handi-
cap is deafness or blindness. I think it's your love.
And pity.
KELLER: Now what does that mean?
ANNIE. All of you here are so sorry for her you've kept
her—like a pet, why, even a dog you housebreak. No
wonder she won't let me come near her. It's useless
for me to try to teach her language or anything else
here. I might as well—
KATE [CUTS IN]: Miss Annie, before you came we spoke
of putting her in an asylum.

(ANNIE *turns back to regard her. A pause.*)

ANNIE: What kind of asylum?
KELLER: For mental defectives.
KATE: I visited there. I can't tell you what I saw, people
like—animals, with—*rats*, in the halls, and—

(*She shakes her head on her vision.*)

What else are we to do, if you give up?

ANNIE: Give up?

KATE: You said it was hopeless.

ANNIE: Here. Give up, why, I only today saw what has to be done, to begin!

(She glances from KATE to KELLER, who stare, waiting; and she makes it as plain and simple as her nervousness permits.)

I—want complete charge of her.

KELLER: You already have that. It has resulted in—

ANNIE: No, I mean day and night. She has to be dependent on me.

KATE: For what?

ANNIE: Everything. The food she eats, the clothes she wears, fresh—

(She is amused at herself, though very serious.)

—air, yes, the air she breathes, whatever her body needs is a—primer, to teach her out of. It's the only way, the one who lets her have it should be her teacher.

(She considers them in turn; they digest it, KELLER frowning, KATE perplexed.)

Not anyone who *loves* her, you have so many feelings they fall over each other like feet, you won't use your chances and you won't let me.

KATE: But if she runs from you—*to* us—

ANNIE: Yes, that's the point. I'll have to live with her somewhere else.

KELLER: What!

ANNIE: Till she learns to depend on and listen to me.

KATE [NOT WITHOUT ALARM]: For how long?

ANNIE: As long as it takes.

(*A pause. She takes a breath.*)

I packed half my things already.

KELLER: Miss—Sullivan!

(*But when* ANNIE *attends upon him he is speechless, and she is merely earnest.*)

ANNIE: Captain Keller, it meets both your conditions. It's the one way I can get back in touch with Helen, and I don't see how I can be rude to you again if you're not around to interfere with me.

KELLER [RED-FACED]: And what is your intention if I say no? Pack the other half, for home, and abandon your charge to—to—

ANNIE: The asylum?

(*She waits, appraises* KELLER's *glare and* KATE's *uncertainty, and decides to use her weapons.*)

I grew up in such an asylum. The state almshouse.

(KATE's *head comes up on this, and* KELLER *stares hard;* ANNIE's *tone is cheerful enough, albeit level as gunfire.*)

Rats—why, my brother Jimmie and I used to play with the rats because we didn't have toys. Maybe you'd like to know what Helen will find there, not on visiting days? One ward was full of the—old women, crippled, blind, most of them dying, but even if what they had was catching there was no-where else to move them, and that's where they put us. There were younger ones across the hall, prostitutes mostly, with T.B., and epileptic fits, and a couple of the kind who—keep after other girls, especially young ones, and some insane. Some just had the D.T.'s. The youngest were in another ward

to have babies they didn't want, they started at
thirteen, fourteen. They'd leave afterwards, but the
babies stayed and we played with them, too, though
a lot of them had—sores all over from diseases you're
not supposed to talk about, but not many of them
lived. The first year we had eighty, seventy died.
The room Jimmie and I played in was the deadhouse,
where they kept the bodies till they could dig—

KATE [CLOSES HER EYES]: Oh, my dear—

ANNIE: —the graves.

(*She is immune to* KATE'*s compassion.*)

No, it made me strong. But I don't think you need
send Helen there. She's strong enough.

(*She waits again; but when neither offers her a
word, she simply concludes.*)

No, I have no conditions, Captain Keller.

KATE [NOT LOOKING UP]: Miss Annie.

ANNIE: Yes.

KATE [A PAUSE]: Where would you—take Helen?

ANNIE: Ohh—

(*Brightly*)

Italy?

KELLER [WHEELING]: What?

ANNIE: Can't have everything, how would this garden
house do? Furnish it, bring Helen here after a long
ride so she won't recognize it, and you can see her
every day. If she doesn't know. Well?

KATE [A SIGH OF RELIEF]: Is that all?

ANNIE: That's all.

KATE: Captain.

(KELLER *turns his head; and* KATE'*s request is quiet
but firm.*)

With your permission?

KELLER [TEETH IN CIGAR]: Why must she depend on you for the food she eats?

ANNIE [A PAUSE]: I want control of it.

KELLER: Why?

ANNIE: It's a way to reach her.

KELLER [STARES]: You intend to *starve* her into letting you touch her?

ANNIE: She won't starve, she'll learn. All's fair in love and war, Captain Keller, you never cut supplies?

KELLER: This is hardly a war!

ANNIE: Well, it's not love. A siege is a siege.

KELLER [HEAVILY]: Miss Sullivan. Do you *like* the child?

ANNIE [STRAIGHT IN HIS EYES]: Do you?

(*A long pause.*)

KATE: You could have a servant here—

ANNIE [AMUSED]: I'll have enough work without looking after a servant! But that boy Percy could sleep here, run errands—

KATE [ALSO AMUSED]: We can let Percy sleep here, I think, Captain?

ANNIE [EAGERLY]: And some old furniture, all our own—

KATE [ALSO EAGER]: Captain? Do you think that walnut bedstead in the barn would be too—

KELLER: I have not yet consented to Percy! Or to the house, or to the proposal! Or to Miss Sullivan's— staying on when I—

(*But he erupts in an irate surrender.*)

Very well, I consent to everything!

(*He shakes the cigar at* ANNIE.)

For two weeks. I'll give you two weeks in this place, and it will be a miracle if you get the child to tolerate you.

KATE: Two weeks? Miss Annie, can you accomplish anything in two weeks?

KELLER: Anything or not, two weeks, then the child comes back to us. Make up your mind, Miss Sullivan, yes or no?

ANNIE: Two weeks. For only one miracle?

(She nods at him, nervously.)

I'll get her to tolerate me.

(KELLER marches out, and slams the door. KATE on her feet regards ANNIE, who is facing the door.)

KATE [THEN]: You can't think as little of love as you said.

(ANNIE glances questioning.)

Or you wouldn't stay.

ANNIE [A PAUSE]: I didn't come here for love. I came for money!

(KATE shakes her head to this, with a smile; after a moment she extends her open hand. ANNIE looks at it, but when she puts hers out it is not to shake hands, it is to set her fist in KATE's palm.)

KATE [PUZZLED]: Hm?

ANNIE: A. It's the first of many. Twenty-six!

(KATE squeezes her fist, squeezes it hard, and hastens out after KELLER. ANNIE stands as the door closes behind her, her manner so apprehensive that finally she slaps her brow, holds it, sighs, and, with her eyes closed, crosses herself for luck.

The lights dim into a cool silhouette scene around her, the lamp paling out, and now, in formal en-

trances, persons appear around ANNIE *with furniture for the room:* PERCY *crosses the stage with a rocking chair and waits;* MARTHA *from another direction bears in a stool,* VINEY *bears in a small table, and the other Negro servant rolls in a bed partway from left; and* ANNIE, *opening her eyes to put her glasses back on, sees them. She turns around in the room once, and goes into action, pointing out locations for each article; the servants place them and leave, and* ANNIE *then darts around, interchanging them. In the midst of this—while* PERCY *and* MARTHA *reappear with a tray of food and a chair, respectively—*JAMES *comes down from the house with* ANNIE'S *suitcase, and stands viewing the room and her quizzically;* ANNIE *halts abruptly under his eyes, embarrassed, then seizes the suitcase from his hand, explaining herself brightly.)*

ANNIE: I always wanted to live in a doll's house!

(She sets the suitcase out of the way, and continues; VINEY *at left appears to position a rod with drapes for a doorway, and the other servant at center pushes in a wheelbarrow loaded with a couple of boxes of* HELEN'S *toys and clothes.* ANNIE *helps lift them into the room, and the servant pushes the wheelbarrow off. In none of this is any heed taken of the imaginary walls of the garden house, the furniture is moved in from every side and itself defines the walls.*

ANNIE *now drags the box of toys into center, props up the doll conspicuously on top; with the people melted away, except for* JAMES, *all is again still. The lights turn again without pause, rising warmer.)*

JAMES: You don't let go of things easily, do you? How will you—win her hand now, in this place?

ANNIE [CURTLY]: Do I know? I lost my temper, and here we are!

JAMES [LIGHTLY]: No touching, no teaching. Of course, you *are* bigger—

ANNIE: I'm not counting on force, I'm counting on her. That little imp is dying to know.

JAMES: Know what?

ANNIE: Anything. Any and every crumb in God's creation. I'll have to use that appetite too.

(*She gives the room a final survey, straightens the bed, arranges the curtains.*)

JAMES [A PAUSE]: Maybe she'll teach you.

ANNIE: Of course.

JAMES: That she isn't. That there's such a thing as—dullness of heart. Acceptance. And letting go. Sooner or later we all give up, don't we?

ANNIE: Maybe you all do. It's my idea of the original sin.

JAMES: What is?

ANNIE [WITHERINGLY]: Giving up.

JAMES [NETTLED]: You won't open her. Why can't you let her be? Have some—pity on her, for being what she is—

ANNIE: If I'd ever once thought like that, I'd be dead!

JAMES [PLEASANTLY]: You will be. Why trouble?

(ANNIE *turns to glare at him; he is mocking.*)

Or will you teach me?

(*And with a bow, he drifts off.*

Now in the distance there comes the clopping of hoofs, drawing near, and nearer, up to the door; and they halt. ANNIE *wheels to face the door. When it opens this time, the* KELLERS—KATE *in travelling bonnet,* KELLER *also hatted—are standing there with*

HELEN *between them; she is in a cloak.* KATE *gently cues her into the room.* HELEN *comes in groping, baffled, but interested in the new surroundings;* ANNIE *evades her exploring hand, her gaze not leaving the child.)*

ANNIE: Does she know where she is?
KATE [SHAKES HER HEAD]: We rode her out in the country for two hours.
KELLER: For all she knows, she could be in another town—

*(*HELEN *stumbles over the box on the floor and in it discovers her doll and other battered toys, is pleased, sits to them, then becomes puzzled and suddenly very wary. She scrambles up and back to her mother's thighs, but* ANNIE *steps in, and it is hers that* HELEN *embraces.* HELEN *recoils, gropes, and touches her cheek instantly.)*

KATE: That's her sign for me.
ANNIE: I know.

*(*HELEN *waits, then recommences her groping, more urgently.* KATE *stands indecisive, and takes an abrupt step toward her, but* ANNIE's *hand is a barrier.)*

In two weeks.
KATE: Miss Annie, I— Please be good to her. These two weeks, try to be very good to her—
ANNIE: I will.

*(*KATE, *turning then, hurries out. The* KELLERS *cross back of the main house.*

ANNIE *closes the door.* HELEN *starts at the door jar, and rushes it.* ANNIE *holds her off.* HELEN *kicks her, breaks free, and careens around the room like an imprisoned bird, colliding with furniture, groping wildly, repeatedly touching her cheek in a growing panic. When she has covered the room, she commences her weird screaming.* ANNIE *moves to comfort her, but her touch sends* HELEN *into a paroxysm of rage: she tears away, falls over her box of toys, flings its contents in handfuls in* ANNIE'S *direction, flings the box too, reels to her feet, rips curtains from the window, bangs and kicks at the door, sweeps objects off the mantelpiece and shelf, a little tornado incarnate, all destruction, until she comes upon her doll and, in the act of hurling it, freezes. Then she clutches it to herself, and in exhaustion sinks sobbing to the floor.* ANNIE *stands contemplating her, in some awe.)*

Two weeks.

(She shakes her head, not without a touch of disgusted bewilderment.)

What did I get into now?

(The lights have been dimming throughout, and the garden house is lit only by moonlight now, with ANNIE *lost in the patches of dark.*

KATE, *now hatless and coatless, enters the family room by the rear door, carrying a lamp.* KELLER, *also hatless, wanders simultaneously around the back of the main house to where* JAMES *has been waiting, in the rising moonlight, on the porch.)*

KELLER: I can't understand it. I had every intention of dismissing that girl, not setting her up like an empress.
JAMES: Yes, what's her secret, sir?
KELLER: Secret?
JAMES [PLEASANTLY]: That enables her to get anything she wants out of you? When I can't.

(JAMES *turns to go into the house, but* KELLER *grasps his wrist, twisting him half to his knees.* KATE *comes from the porch.*)

KELLER [ANGRILY]: She does *not* get anything she—
JAMES [IN PAIN]: Don't—don't—
KATE: Captain.
KELLER: He's afraid.

(*He throws* JAMES *away from him, with contempt.*)

What *does* he want out of me?
JAMES [AN OUTCRY]: My God, don't you know?

(*He gazes from* KELLER *to* KATE.)

Everything you forgot, when you forgot my mother.
KELLER: What!

(JAMES *wheels into the house.* KELLER *takes a stride to the porch, to roar after him.*)

One thing that girl's secret is not, she doesn't fire one shot and disappear!

(KATE *stands rigid, and* KELLER *comes back to her.*)

Katie. Don't mind what he—
KATE: Captain, *I* am proud of you.
KELLER: For what?
KATE: For letting this girl have what she needs.
KELLER: Why can't my son be? He can't bear me, you'd think I treat him as hard as this girl does Helen—

(*He breaks off, as it dawns in him.*)

KATE [GENTLY]: Perhaps you do.
KELLER: But he has to learn some respect!

KATE [A PAUSE, WRYLY]: *Do* you like the child?

(*She turns again to the porch, but pauses, reluctant.*)

How empty the house is, tonight.

(*After a moment she continues on in.* KELLER *stands moveless, as the moonlight dies on him.*

The distant belfry chimes toll, two o'clock, and with them, a moment later, comes the boy's voice on the wind, in a whisper:)

BOY'S VOICE: Annie. Annie.

(*In her patch of dark* ANNIE, *now in her nightgown, hurls a cup into a corner as though it were her grief, getting rid of its taste through her teeth.*)

ANNIE: No! No pity, I won't have it.

(*She comes to* HELEN, *prone on the floor.*)

On either of us.

(*She goes to her knees, but when she touches* HELEN'*s hand the child starts up awake, recoils, and scrambles away from her under the bed.* ANNIE *stares after her. She strikes her palm on the floor, with passion.*)

I *will* touch you!

(*She gets to her feet, and paces in a kind of anger around the bed, her hand in her hair, and confronting* HELEN *at each turn.*)

How, how? How do I—

(ANNIE *stops. Then she calls out urgently, loudly.*)

Percy! Percy!

(*She moves swiftly to the drapes, at left.*)

Percy, wake up!

(PERCY'S *voice comes in a thick sleepy mumble, un-intelligible.*)

Get out of bed and come in here, I need you.

(ANNIE *darts away, finds and strikes a match, and touches it to the hanging lamp; the lights come up dimly in the room, and* PERCY *stands bare to the waist in torn overalls between the drapes, with eyes closed, swaying.* ANNIE *goes to him, pats his cheeks vigorously.*)

Percy. You awake?
PERCY: No'm.
ANNIE: How would you like to play a nice game?
PERCY: Whah?
ANNIE: With Helen. She's under the bed. Touch her hand.

(*She kneels* PERCY *down at the bed, thrusting his hand under it to contact* HELEN'S; HELEN *emits an animal sound and crawls to the opposite side, but commences sniffing.* ANNIE *rounds the bed with* PERCY *and thrusts his hand again at* HELEN; *this time* HELEN *clutches it, sniffs in recognition, and comes scrambling out after* PERCY, *to hug him with delight.* PERCY *alarmed struggles, and* HELEN'S *fingers go to his mouth.*)

PERCY: Lemme go. Lemme go—

(HELEN *fingers her own lips, as before, moving them in dumb imitation.*)

She tryin' talk. She gonna hit me—

ANNIE [GRIMLY]: She *can* talk. If she only knew, I'll show you how. She makes letters.

(*She opens* PERCY's *other hand, and spells into it:*)

This one is C. C.

(*She hits his palm with it a couple of times, her eyes upon* HELEN *across him;* HELEN *gropes to feel what* PERCY's *hand is doing, and when she encounters* ANNIE's *she falls back from them.*)

She's mad at me now, though, she won't play. But she knows lots of letters. Here's another, A. C, a. C, a.

(*But she is watching* HELEN, *who comes groping, consumed with curiosity;* ANNIE *makes the letters in* PERCY's *hand, and* HELEN *pokes to question what they are up to. Then* HELEN *snatches* PERCY's *other hand, and quickly spells four letters into it.* ANNIE *follows them aloud.*)

C, a, k, e! She spells cake, she gets cake.

(*She is swiftly over to the tray of food, to fetch cake and a jug of milk.*)

She doesn't know yet it means this. Isn't it funny she knows how to spell it and doesn't *know* she knows?

(*She breaks the cake in two pieces, and extends one to each;* HELEN *rolls away from her offer.*)

Well, if she won't play it with me, I'll play it with you. Would you like to learn one she doesn't know?

PERCY: No'm.

(*But* ANNIE *seizes his wrist, and spells to him.*)

ANNIE: M, i, l, k. M is this. I, that's an easy one, just the little finger. L is this—

(*And* HELEN *comes back with her hand, to feel the new word.* ANNIE *brushes her away, and continues spelling aloud to* PERCY. HELEN's *hand comes back again, and tries to get in;* ANNIE *brushes it away again.* HELEN's *hand insists, and* ANNIE *puts it away rudely.*)

No, why should I talk to you? I'm teaching Percy a new word. L. K is this—

(HELEN *now yanks their hands apart; she butts* PERCY *away, and thrusts her palm out insistently.* ANNIE's *eyes are bright, with glee.*)

Ho, you're *jealous,* are you!

(HELEN's *hand waits, intractably waits.*)

All *right.*

(ANNIE *spells into it,* milk; *and* HELEN *after a moment spells it back to* ANNIE. ANNIE *takes her hand, with her whole face shining. She gives a great sigh.*)

Good! So I'm finally back to where I can touch you, hm? Touch and go! No love lost, but here we go.

(*She puts the jug of milk into* HELEN's *hand and squeezes* PERCY's *shoulder.*)

You can go to bed now, you've earned your sleep. Thank you.

(PERCY *stumbling up weaves his way out through the drapes.* HELEN *finishes drinking, and holds the jug out, for* ANNIE; *when* ANNIE *takes it,* HELEN *crawls onto the bed, and makes for sleep.* ANNIE *stands, looks down at her.)*

Now all I have to teach you is—one word. Everything.

(She sets the jug down. On the floor now ANNIE *spies the doll, stoops to pick it up, and with it dangling in her hand, turns off the lamp. A shaft of moonlight is left on* HELEN *in the bed, and a second shaft on the rocking chair; and* ANNIE, *after putting off her smoked glasses, sits in the rocker with the doll. She is rather happy, and dangles the doll on her knee, and it makes its momma sound.* ANNIE *whispers to it in mock solicitude.)*

Hush, little baby. Don't—say a word—

(She lays it against her shoulder, and begins rocking with it, patting its diminutive behind; she talks the lullaby to it, humorously at first.)

  Momma's gonna buy you—a mockingbird:
    If that—mockingbird don't sing—

(The rhythm of the rocking takes her into the tune, softly, and more tenderly.)

  Momma's gonna buy you a diamond ring:
    If that diamond ring turns to brass—

(A third shaft of moonlight outside now rises to pick out JAMES *at the main house, with one foot on the porch step; he turns his body, as if hearing the song.)*

  Momma's gonna buy you a looking-glass:
    If that looking-glass gets broke—

(In the family room a fourth shaft picks out KELLER

seated at the table, in thought; and he, too, lifts his head, as if hearing.)

    Momma's gonna buy you a billy goat:
    If that billy goat won't pull—

(The fifth shaft is upstairs in ANNIE'S *room, and picks out* KATE, *pacing there; and she halts, turning her head, too, as if hearing.)*

    Momma's gonna buy you a cart and bull:
    If that cart and bull turns over,
    Momma's gonna buy you a dog named Rover;
    If that dog named Rover won't bark—

(With the shafts of moonlight on HELEN, *and* JAMES, *and* KELLER, *and* KATE, *all moveless, and* ANNIE *rocking the doll, the curtain ends the act.)*

ACT III

The stage is totally dark, until we see ANNIE *and* HELEN *silhouetted on the bed in the garden house.* ANNIE'S *voice is audible, very patient, and worn; it has been saying this for a long time.*

ANNIE: Water, Helen. This is water. W, a, t, e, r. It has a *name.*

(*A silence. Then:*)

Egg, e, g, g. It has a *name*, the name stands for the thing. Oh, it's so simple, simple as birth, to explain.

(*The lights have commenced to rise, not on the garden house but on the homestead. Then:*)

Helen, Helen, the chick *has* to come out of its shell, sometime. You come out, too.

(*In the bedroom upstairs, we see* VINEY *unhurriedly washing the window, dusting, turning the mattress, readying the room for use again; then in the family room a diminished group at one end of the table—* KATE, KELLER, JAMES—*finishing up a quiet breakfast; then outside, down right, the other Negro servant on his knees, assisted by* MARTHA, *working with a trowel around a new trellis and wheelbarrow. The scene is one of everyday calm, and all are oblivious to* ANNIE'S *voice.*)

There's only one way out, for you, and it's language. To learn that your fingers can talk. And say anything,

anything you can name. This is mug. Mug, m, u, g.
Helen, it has a *name*. It—has—a—*name*—

(KATE *rises from the table.*)

KELLER [GENTLY]: You haven't eaten, Katie.
KATE [SMILES, SHAKES HER HEAD]: I haven't the appetite.
I'm too—restless, I can't sit to it.
KELLER: You should eat, my dear. It will be a long day,
waiting.
JAMES [LIGHTLY]: But it's been a short two weeks. I
never thought life could be so—noiseless, went much
too quickly for me.

(KATE *and* KELLER *gaze at him, in silence.* JAMES
becomes uncomfortable.)

ANNIE: C, a, r, d. Card. C, a—
JAMES. Well, the house has been practically normal,
hasn't it?
KELLER [HARSHLY]: Jimmie.
JAMES: Is it wrong to enjoy a quiet breakfast, after five
years? And you two even seem to enjoy each other—
KELLER: It could be even more noiseless, Jimmie, without
your tongue running every minute. Haven't you
enough feeling to imagine what Katie has been under-
going, ever since—

(KATE *stops him, with her hand on his arm.*)

KATE: Captain.

(*To* JAMES.)

It's true. The two weeks have been normal, quiet, all
you say. But not short. Interminable.

(*She rises, and wanders out; she pauses on the porch
steps, gazing toward the garden house.*)

ANNIE [FADING]: W, a, t, e, r. But it means *this*. W, a, t, e, r. *This*. W, a, t—

JAMES: I only meant that Miss Sullivan is a boon. Of contention, though, it seems.

KELLER [HEAVILY]: If and when you're a parent, Jimmie, you will understand what separation means. A mother loses a—protector.

JAMES [BAFFLED]: Hm?

KELLER: You'll learn, we don't just keep our children safe. They keep us safe.

(*He rises, with his empty coffee cup and saucer.*)

There are of course all kinds of separation, Katie has lived with one kind for five years. And another is disappointment. In a child.

(*He goes with the cup out the rear door.* JAMES *sits for a long moment of stillness. In the garden house the lights commence to come up;* ANNIE, *haggard at the table, is writing a letter, her face again almost in contact with the stationery;* HELEN, *apart on the stool, and for the first time as clean and neat as a button, is quietly crocheting an endless chain of wool, which snakes all around the room.*)

ANNIE: "I, feel, every, day, more, and, more, in—"

(*She pauses, and turns the pages of a dictionary open before her; her finger descends the words to a full stop. She elevates her eyebrows, then copies the word.*)

"—adequate."

(*In the main house* JAMES *pushes up, and goes to the front doorway, after* KATE.)

JAMES: Kate?

(KATE *turns her glance.* JAMES *is rather weary.*)

I'm sorry. Open my mouth, like that fairy tale, frogs
jump out.
KATE: No. It has been better. For everyone.

(*She starts away, up center.*)

ANNIE [WRITING]: "If, only, there, were, someone, to,
help, me, I, need, a, teacher, as, much, as, Helen—"
JAMES: Kate.

(KATE *halts, waits.*)

What does he want from me?
KATE: That's not the question. Stand up to the world,
Jimmie, that comes first.
JAMES [A PAUSE, WRYLY]: But the world is him.
KATE: Yes. And no one can do it for you.
JAMES: Kate.

(*His voice is humble.*)

At least we— Could you—be my friend?
KATE: I am.

(KATE *turns to wander, up back of the garden house.*
ANNIE'S *murmur comes at once; the lights begin to die
on the main house.*)

ANNIE: "—my, mind, is, undisiplined, full, of, skips, and,
jumps, and—"

(*She halts, rereads, frowns.*)

Hm.

(ANNIE *puts her nose again in the dictionary, flips
back to an earlier page, and fingers down the words;*

KATE *presently comes down toward the bay window
with a trayful of food.)*

Disinter—disinterested—disjoin—dis—

(She backtracks, indignant.)

Disinterested, disjoin— Where's disipline?

*(She goes a page or two back, searching with her
finger, muttering.)*

What a dictionary, have to know how to spell it before
you can look up how to spell it, disciple, *disciplinel*
Diskipline.

(She corrects the word in her letter.)

Undisciplined.

*(But her eyes are bothering her, she closes them in
exhaustion and gently fingers the eyelids.* KATE *watches
her through the window.)*

KATE: What are you doing to your eyes?

*(*ANNIE *glances around; she puts her smoked glasses
on, and gets up to come over, assuming a cheerful
energy.)*

ANNIE: It's worse on my vanity! I'm learning to spell. It's
   like a surprise party, the most unexpected characters
   turn up.
KATE: You're not to overwork your eyes, Miss Annie.
ANNIE: Well.

*(She takes the tray, sets it on her chair, and carries
chair and tray to* HELEN.*)*

Whatever I spell to Helen I'd better spell right.

KATE [ALMOST WISTFUL]: How—serene she is.

ANNIE: She learned this stitch yesterday. Now I can't get her to stop!

(*She disentangles one foot from the wool chain, and sets the chair before* HELEN. HELEN *at its contact with her knee feels the plate, promptly sets her crocheting down, and tucks the napkin in at her neck, but* ANNIE *withholds the spoon; when* HELEN *finds it missing, she folds her hands in her lap, and quietly waits.* ANNIE *twinkles at* KATE *with mock devoutness.*)

Such a little lady, she'd sooner starve than eat with her fingers.

(*She gives* HELEN *the spoon, and* HELEN *begins to eat, neatly.*)

KATE: You've taught her so much, these two weeks. I would never have—

ANNIE: Not enough.

(*She is suddenly gloomy, shakes her head.*)

Obedience isn't enough. Well, she learned two nouns this morning, key and water, brings her up to eighteen nouns and three verbs.

KATE [HESITANT]: But—not—

ANNIE: No. Not that they mean things. It's still a finger-game, no meaning.

(*She turns to* KATE, *abruptly.*)

Mrs. Keller—

(*But she defers it; she comes back, to sit in the bay and lift her hand.*)

Shall we play our finger-game?
KATE: How will she learn it?
ANNIE: It will come.

(*She spells a word;* KATE *does not respond.*)

KATE: How?
ANNIE [A PAUSE]: How does a bird learn to fly?

(*She spells again.*)

We're born to use words, like wings, it has to come.
KATE: How?
ANNIE [ANOTHER PAUSE, WEARILY]: All right. I don't
know how.

(*She pushes up her glasses, to rub her eyes.*)

I've done everything I could think of. Whatever she's
learned here—keeping herself clean, knitting, string-
ing beads, meals, setting-up exercises each morning,
we climb trees, hunt eggs, yesterday a chick was born
in her hands—all of it I spell, everything we do, we
never stop spelling. I go to bed with—writer's cramp
from talking so much!
KATE: I worry about you, Miss Annie. You must rest.
ANNIE: Now? She spells back in her *sleep,* her fingers
make letters when she doesn't know! In her bones
those five fingers know, that hand aches to—speak out,
and something in her mind is asleep, how do I—nudge
that awake? That's the one question.
KATE: With no answer.
ANNIE [LONG PAUSE]: Except keep at it. Like this.

(*She again begins spelling—I, need—and* KATE'S *brows
gather, following the words.*)

KATE: More—time?

(*She glances at* ANNIE, *who looks her in the eyes, silent.*)

Here?
ANNIE: Spell it.

(KATE *spells a word—no—shaking her head;* ANNIE *spells two words—why, not—back, with an impatient question in her eyes; and* KATE *moves her head in pain to answer it.*)

KATE: Because I can't—

ANNIE: Spell it! If she ever learns, you'll have a lot to tell each other, start now.

(KATE *painstakingly spells in air. In the midst of this the rear door opens, and* KELLER *enters with the setter* BELLE *in tow.*)

KELLER: Miss Sullivan? On my way to the office, I brought Helen a playmate—
ANNIE: Outside please, Captain Keller.
KELLER: My dear child, the two weeks are up today, surely you don't object to—
ANNIE [RISING]: They're not up till six o'clock.
KELLER [INDULGENT]: Oh, now. What difference can a fraction of one day—
ANNIE: An agreement is an agreement. Now you've been very good, I'm sure you can keep it up for a few more hours.

(*She escorts* KELLER *by the arm over the threshold; he obeys, leaving* BELLE.)

KELLER: Miss Sullivan, you are a tyrant.
ANNIE: Likewise, I'm sure. You can stand there, and close the door if she comes.

KATE: I don't think you know how eager we are to have
    her back in our arms—

ANNIE: I do know, it's my main worry.

KELLER: It's like expecting a new child in the house.
    Well, she *is*, so—composed, so—

(*Gently*)

Attractive. You've done wonders for her, Miss Sullivan.

ANNIE [NOT A QUESTION]: Have I.

KELLER: If there's anything you want from us in repay-
    ment tell us, it will be a privilege to—

ANNIE: I just told Mrs. Keller. I want more time.

KATE: Miss Annie—

ANNIE: Another week.

(HELEN *lifts her head, and begins to sniff.*)

KELLER: We miss the child. *I* miss her, I'm glad to say,
    that's a different debt I owe you—

ANNIE: Pay it to Helen. Give *her* another week.

KATE [GENTLY]: Doesn't she miss us?

KELLER: Of course she does. What a wrench this unex-
    plainable—exile must be to her, can you say it's not?

ANNIE: No. But I—

(HELEN *is off the stool, to grope about the room; when
she encounters* BELLE, *she throws her arms around
the dog's neck in delight.*)

KATE: Doesn't she need affection too, Miss Annie?

ANNIE [WAVERING]: She—never shows me she needs it,
    she won't have any—caressing or—

KATE: But you're not her mother.

KELLER: And what would another week accomplish? We
    are more than satisfied, you've done more than we
    ever thought possible, taught her constructive—

ANNIE: I can't promise anything. All I can—

KELLER [NO BREAK]: —things to do, to behave like—even

look like—a human child, so manageable, contented, cleaner, more—

ANNIE [WITHERING]: Cleaner.

KELLER: Well. We say cleanliness is next to godliness, Miss—

ANNIE: Cleanliness is next to nothing, she has to learn that everything has its name! That words can be her *eyes*, to everything in the world outside her, and inside too, what is she without words? With them she can think, have ideas, be reached, there's not a thought or fact in the world that can't be hers. You publish a newspaper, Captain Keller, do I have to tell you what words are? And she has them already—

KELLER: Miss Sullivan.

ANNIE: —eighteen nouns and three verbs, they're in her fingers now, I need only time to push *one* of them into her mind! One, and everything under the sun will follow. Don't you see what she's learned here is only clearing the way for that? I can't risk her unlearning it, give me more time alone with her, another week to—

KELLER: Look.

(*He points, and* ANNIE *turns.* HELEN *is playing with* BELLE's *claws; she makes letters with her fingers, shows them to* BELLE, *waits with her palm, then manipulates the dog's claws.*)

What is she spelling?

(*A silence.*)

KATE: Water?

(ANNIE *nods.*)

KELLER: Teaching a dog to spell.

(*A pause.*)

The dog doesn't know what she means, any more
than she knows what you mean, Miss Sullivan. I
think you ask too much, of her and yourself. God
may not have meant Helen to have the—eyes you
speak of.

ANNIE [TONELESS]: I mean her to.

KELLER [CURIOUSLY]: What is it to you?

(ANNIE's *head comes slowly up.*)

You make us see how we indulge her for our sake.
Is the opposite true, for you?

ANNIE [THEN]: Half a week?

KELLER: An agreement *is* an agreement.

ANNIE: Mrs. Keller?

KATE [SIMPLY]: I want her back.

(A wait; ANNIE *then lets her hands drop in surrender,
and nods.*)

KELLER: I'll send Viney over to help you pack.

ANNIE: Not until six o'clock. I have her till six o'clock.

KELLER [CONSENTING]: Six o'clock. Come, Katie.

(KATE *leaving the window joins him around back,
while* KELLER *closes the door; they are shut out.*

*Only the garden house is daylit now, and the light on
it is narrowing down.* ANNIE *stands watching* HELEN
work BELLE's *claws. Then she settles beside them on
her knees, and stops* HELEN's *hand.*)

ANNIE [GENTLY]: No.

(*She shakes her head, with* HELEN's *hand to her face,
then spells.*)

Dog. D, o, g. Dog.

(She touches HELEN's *hand to* BELLE. HELEN *dutifully pats the dog's head, and resumes spelling to its paw.)*

Not water.

*(*ANNIE *rolls to her feet, brings a tumbler of water back from the tray, and kneels with it, to seize* HELEN's *hand and spell.)*

Here. Water. *Water.*

(She thrusts HELEN's *hand into the tumbler.* HELEN *lifts her hand out dripping, wipes it daintily on* BELLE's *hide, and taking the tumbler from* ANNIE, *endeavors to thrust* BELLE's *paw into it.* ANNIE *sits watching, wearily.)*

I don't know how to tell you. Not a soul in the world knows how to tell you. Helen, Helen.

(She bends in compassion to touch her lips to HELEN's *temple, and instantly* HELEN *pauses, her hands off the dog, her head slightly averted. The lights are still narrowing, and* BELLE *slinks off. After a moment* ANNIE *sits back.)*

Yes, what's it to me? They're satisfied. Give them back their child and dog, both housebroken, everyone's satisfied. But me, and you.

*(*HELEN's *hand comes out into the light, groping.)*

Reach. *Reach!*

*(*ANNIE *extending her own hand grips* HELEN's; *the two hands are clasped, tense in the light, the rest of the room changing in shadow.)*

I wanted to teach you—oh, everything the earth is

full of, Helen, everything on it that's ours for a wink
and it's gone, and what we are on it, the—light we
bring to it and leave behind in—words, why, you
can see five thousand years back in a light of words,
everything we feel, think, know—and share, in words,
so not a soul is in darkness, or done with, even in
the grave. And I know, I *know*, one word and I can
—put the world in your hand—and whatever it is to
me, I won't take less! How, how, how do I tell you
that *this*—

(She spells.)

—means a *word*, and the word means this *thing*,
wool?

(She thrusts the wool at HELEN's *hand;* HELEN *sits,
puzzled.* ANNIE *puts the crocheting aside.)*

Or this—s, t, o, o, l—means this *thing*, stool?

(She claps HELEN's *palm to the stool.* HELEN *waits,
uncomprehending.* ANNIE *snatches up her napkin,
spells:)*

Napkin!

(She forces it on HELEN's *hand, waits, discards it,
lifts a fold of the child's dress, spells:)*

Dress!

(She lets it drop, spells:)

F, a, c, e, face!

(She draws HELEN's *hand to her cheek, and pressing
it there, staring into the child's responseless eyes, hears*

*the distant belfry begin to toll, slowly: one, two, three,
four, five, six.*

*On the third stroke the lights stealing in around the
garden house show us figures waiting:* VINEY, *the other
servant,* MARTHA, PERCY *at the drapes, and* JAMES
on the dim porch. ANNIE *and* HELEN *remain, frozen.
The chimes die away. Silently* PERCY *moves the drape-
rod back out of sight;* VINEY *steps into the room—not
using the door—and unmakes the bed; the other servant brings the wheelbarrow over, leaves it handy, rolls
the bed off;* VINEY *puts the bed linens on top of a
waiting boxful of* HELEN'S *toys, and loads the box on
the wheelbarrow;* MARTHA *and* PERCY *take out the
chairs, with the trayful, then the table; and* JAMES,
coming down and into the room, lifts ANNIE'S *suitcase
from its corner.* VINEY *and the other servant load the
remaining odds and ends on the wheelbarrow, and
the servant wheels it off.* VINEY *and the children de-
parting leave only* JAMES *in the room with* ANNIE *and
HELEN.* JAMES *studies the two of them, without mockery, and then, quietly going to the door and opening
it, bears the suitcase out, and housewards. He leaves
the door open.*

KATE *steps into the doorway, and stands.* ANNIE *lifting
her gaze from* HELEN *sees her; she takes* HELEN'S *hand
from her cheek, and returns it to the child's own,
stroking it there twice, in her mother-sign, before
spelling slowly into it:)*

M, o, t, h, e, r. Mother.

(HELEN *with her hand free strokes her cheek, suddenly forlorn.* ANNIE *takes her hand again.)*

M, o, t, h—

(*But* KATE *is trembling with such impatience that her voice breaks from her, harsh.*)

KATE: Let her *come!*

(ANNIE *lifts* HELEN *to her feet, with a turn, and gives her a little push. Now* HELEN *begins groping, sensing something, trembling herself; and* KATE *falling one step in onto her knees clasps her, kissing her.* HELEN *clutches her, tight as she can.* KATE *is inarticulate, choked, repeating* HELEN'S *name again and again. She wheels with her in her arms, to stumble away out the doorway;* ANNIE *stands unmoving, while* KATE *in a blind walk carries* HELEN *like a baby behind the main house, out of view.*

ANNIE *is now alone on the stage. She turns, gazing around at the stripped room, bidding it silently farewell, impassively, like a defeated general on the deserted battlefield. All that remains is a stand with a basin of water; and here* ANNIE *takes up an eyecup, bathes each of her eyes, empties the eyecup, drops it in her purse, and tiredly locates her smoked glasses on the floor. The lights alter subtly; in the act of putting on her glasses* ANNIE *hears something that stops her, with head lifted. We hear it too, the voices out of the past, including her own now, in a whisper:*)

BOY'S VOICE: You said we'd be together, forever— You promised, forever and—*Annie!*

ANAGNOS' VOICE: But that battle is dead and done with, why not let it stay buried?

ANNIE'S VOICE [WHISPERING]: I think God must owe me a resurrection.

ANAGNOS' VOICE: What?

(*A pause, and* ANNIE *answers it herself, heavily.*)

ANNIE: And I owe God one.

BOY'S VOICE: Forever and ever—

   (ANNIE *shakes her head.*)

   —forever, and ever, and—

   (ANNIE *covers her ears.*)

   —forever, and ever, and ever—

   (*It pursues* ANNIE; *she flees to snatch up her purse,
   wheels to the doorway, and* KELLER *is standing in it.
   The lights have lost their special color.*)

KELLER: Miss—Annie.

   (*He has an envelope in his fingers.*)

   I've been waiting to give you this.
ANNIE [AFTER A BREATH]: What?
KELLER: Your first month's salary.

   (*He puts it in her hand.*)

   With many more to come, I trust. It doesn't express
   what we feel, it doesn't pay our debt. For what you've
   done.
ANNIE: What have I done?
KELLER: Taken a wild thing, and given us back a child.
ANNIE [PRESENTLY]: I taught her one thing, no. Don't
   do this, don't do that—
KELLER: It's more than all of us could, in all the years
   we—
ANNIE: I wanted to teach her what language is. I wanted
   to teach her yes.
KELLER: You will have time.
ANNIE: I don't know how. I know without it to do
   nothing but obey is—no gift, obedience without

understanding is a—blindness, too. Is that all I've
wished on her?

KELLER [GENTLY]: No, no—

ANNIE: Maybe. I don't know what else to do. Simply
go on, keep doing what I've done, and have—faith
that inside she's— That inside it's waiting. Like water,
underground. All I can do is keep on.

KELLER: It's enough. For us.

ANNIE: You can help, Captain Keller.

KELLER: How?

ANNIE: Even learning no has been at a cost. Of much
trouble and pain. Don't undo it.

KELLER: Why should we wish to—

ANNIE [ABRUPTLY]: The world isn't an easy place for
anyone, I don't want her just to obey but to let her
have her way in everything is a lie, to *her*, I can't—

(*Her eyes fill, it takes her by surprise, and she laughs
through it.*)

And I don't even love her, she's not my child! Well.
You've got to stand between that lie and her.

KELLER: We'll try.

ANNIE: Because *I* will. As long as you let me stay, that's
one promise I'll keep.

KELLER: Agreed. We've learned something too, I hope.

(*A pause*)

Won't you come now, to supper?

ANNIE: Yes.

(*She wags the envelope, ruefully.*)

Why doesn't God pay His debts each month?

KELLER: I beg your pardon?

ANNIE: Nothing. I used to wonder how I could—

(The lights are fading on them, simultaneously rising on the family room of the main house, where VINEY is polishing glassware at the table set for dinner.)

—earn a living.

KELLER: Oh, you do.

ANNIE: I really do. Now the question is, can I survive it!

(KELLER smiles, offers his arm.)

KELLER: May I?

(ANNIE takes it, and the lights lose them as he escorts her out.

Now in the family room the rear door opens, and HELEN steps in. She stands a moment, then sniffs in one deep grateful breath, and her hands go out vigorously to familiar things, over the door panels, and to the chairs around the table, and over the silverware on the table, until she mets VINEY; she pats her flank approvingly.)

VINEY: Oh, we glad to have you back too, prob'ly.

(HELEN hurries groping to the front door, opens and closes it, removes its key, opens and closes it again to be sure it is unlocked, gropes back to the rear door and repeats the procedure, removing its key and hugging herself gleefully.

AUNT EV is next in by the rear door, with a relish tray; she bends to kiss HELEN's cheek. HELEN finds KATE behind her, and thrusts the keys at her.)

KATE: What? Oh.

(To EV)

Keys.

(*She pockets them, lets* HELEN *feel them.*)

Yes, I'll keep the keys. I think we've had enough of locked doors, too.

(JAMES, *having earlier put* ANNIE's *suitcase inside her door upstairs and taken himself out of view around the corner, now reappears and comes down the stairs as* ANNIE *and* KELLER *mount the porch steps. Following them into the family room, he pats* ANNIE's *hair in passing, rather to her surprise.*)

JAMES: Evening, general.

(*He takes his own chair opposite.*

VINEY *bears the empty water pitcher out to the porch. The remaining suggestion of garden house is gone now, and the water pump is unobstructed;* VINEY *pumps water into the pitcher.*

KATE *surveying the table breaks the silence.*)

KATE: Will you say grace, Jimmie?

(*They bow their heads, except for* HELEN, *who palms her empty plate and then reaches to be sure her mother is there.* JAMES *considers a moment, glances across at* ANNIE, *lowers his head again, and obliges.*)

JAMES [LIGHTLY]: And Jacob was left alone, and wrestled with an angel until the breaking of the day; and the hollow of Jacob's thigh was out of joint, as he wrestled with him; and the angel said, Let me go, for the day breaketh. And Jacob said, I will not let thee go, except thou bless me. Amen.

(ANNIE *has lifted her eyes suspiciously at* JAMES, *who winks expressionlessly and inclines his head to* HELEN.)

Oh, you angel.

(*The others lift their faces;* VINEY *returns with the pitcher, setting it down near* KATE, *then goes out the rear door; and* ANNIE *puts a napkin around* HELEN.)

AUNT EV: That's a very strange grace, James.

KELLER: Will you start the muffins, Ev?

JAMES: It's from the Good Book, isn't it?

AUNT EV [PASSING A PLATE]: Well, of course it is. Didn't you know?

JAMES: Yes, I knew.

KELLER [SERVING]: Ham, Miss Annie?

ANNIE: Please.

AUNT EV: Then why ask?

JAMES: I meant it *is* from the Good Book, and therefore a fitting grace.

AUNT EV: Well. I don't know about *that.*

KATE [WITH THE PITCHER]: Miss Annie?

ANNIE: Thank you.

AUNT EV: There's an awful *lot* of things in the Good Book that I wouldn't care to hear just before eating.

(*When* ANNIE *reaches for the pitcher,* HELEN *removes her napkin and drops it to the floor.* ANNIE *is filling* HELEN's *glass when she notices it; she considers* HELEN's *bland expression a moment, then bends, retrieves it, and tucks it around* HELEN's *neck again.*)

JAMES: Well, fitting in the sense that Jacob's thigh was out of joint, and so is this piggie's.

AUNT EV: I declare, James—

KATE: Pickles, Aunt Ev?

AUNT EV: Oh, I should say so, you know my opinion of your pickles—

KATE: This is the end of them, I'm afraid. I didn't put up nearly enough last summer, this year I intend to—

(*She interrupts herself, seeing* HELEN *deliberately lift off her napkin and drop it again to the floor. She bends to retrieve it, but* ANNIE *stops her arm.*)

KELLER [NOT NOTICING]: Reverend looked in at the office today to complain his hens have stopped laying. Poor fellow, *he* was out of joint, all he could—

(*He stops too, to frown down the table at* KATE, HELEN, *and* ANNIE *in turn, all suspended in mid-motion.*)

JAMES [NOT NOTICING]: I've always suspected those hens.
AUNT EV: Of what?
JAMES: I think they're Papist. Has he tried—

(*He stops, too, following* KELLER's *eyes.* ANNIE *now stops to pick the napkin up.*)

AUNT EV: James, now you're pulling my—lower extremity, the first thing you know we'll be—

(*She stops, too, hearing herself in the silence.* ANNIE, *with everyone now watching, for the third time puts the napkin on* HELEN. HELEN *yanks it off, and throws it down.* ANNIE *rises, lifts* HELEN's *plate, and bears it away.* HELEN, *feeling it gone, slides down and commences to kick up under the table; the dishes jump.* ANNIE *contemplates this for a moment, then coming back takes* HELEN's *wrists firmly and swings her off the chair.* HELEN *struggling gets one hand free, and catches at her mother's skirt; when* KATE *takes her by the shoulders,* HELEN *hangs quiet.*)

KATE: Miss Annie.
ANNIE: No.

KATE [A PAUSE]: It's a very special day.

ANNIE [GRIMLY]: It will be, when I give in to that.

(*She tries to disengage* HELEN's *hand;* KATE *lays hers on* ANNIE'S.)

KATE: Please. I've hardly had a chance to welcome her home—

ANNIE: Captain Keller.

KELLER [EMBARRASSED]: Oh. Katie, we—had a little talk, Miss Annie feels that if we indulge Helen in these—

AUNT EV: But what's the child done?

ANNIE: She's learned not to throw things on the floor and kick. It took us the best part of two weeks and—

AUNT EV: But only a napkin, it's not as if it were break-able!

ANNIE: And everything she's learned *is?* Mrs. Keller, I don't think we should—play tug-of-war for her, either give her to me or you keep her from kicking.

KATE: What do you wish to do?

ANNIE: Let me take her from the table.

AUNT EV: Oh, let her stay, my goodness, she's only a child, she doesn't have to wear a napkin if she doesn't want to her first evening—

ANNIE [LEVEL]: And ask outsiders not to interfere.

AUNT EV [ASTONISHED]: Out—outsi— I'm the child's *aunt!*

KATE [DISTRESSED]: Will once hurt so much, Miss Annie? I've—made all Helen's favorite foods, tonight.

(*A pause*)

KELLER [GENTLY]: It's a homecoming party, Miss Annie.

(ANNIE *after a moment releases* HELEN. *But she cannot accept it, at her own chair she shakes her head and turns back, intent on* KATE.)

ANNIE: She's testing you. You realize?

JAMES [TO ANNIE]: She's testing you.

KELLER: Jimmie, be quiet.

(JAMES *sits, tense.*)

Now she's home, naturally she—

ANNIE: And wants to see what will happen. At your hands. I said it was my main worry, is this what you promised me not half an hour ago?

KELLER [REASONABLY]: But she's *not* kicking, now—

ANNIE: And not learning not to. Mrs. Keller, teaching her is bound to be painful, to everyone. I know it hurts to watch, but she'll live up to just what you demand of her, and no more.

JAMES [PALELY]: She's testing *you*.

KELLER [TESTILY]: Jimmie.

JAMES: I have an opinion, I think I should—

KELLER: No one's interested in hearing your opinion.

ANNIE: *I'm* interested, of course she's testing me. Let me keep her to what she's learned and she'll go on learning from me. Take her out of my hands and it all comes apart.

(KATE *closes her eyes, digesting it;* ANNIE *sits again, with a brief comment for her.*)

Be bountiful, it's at her expense.

(*She turns to* JAMES, *flatly.*)

Please pass me more of—her favorite foods.

(*Then* KATE *lifts* HELEN's *hand, and turning her toward* ANNIE, *surrenders her;* HELEN *makes for her own chair.*)

KATE [LOW]: Take her, Miss Annie.

ANNIE [THEN]: Thank you.

(*But the moment* ANNIE *rising reaches for her hand,*

HELEN *begins to fight and kick, clutching to the tablecloth, and uttering laments.* ANNIE *again tries to loosen
her hand, and* KELLER *rises.)*

KELLER [TOLERANT]: I'm afraid you're the difficulty, Miss
Annie. Now I'll keep her to what she's learned,
you're quite right there—

(*He takes* HELEN'S *hands from* ANNIE, *pats them;*
HELEN *quiets down.*)

—but I don't see that we need send her from the
table, after all, she's the guest of honor. Bring her
plate back.

ANNIE: If she was a seeing child, none of you would
tolerate one—

KELLER: Well, she's not, I think some compromise is
called for. Bring her plate, please.

(ANNIE'S *jaw sets, but she restores the plate, while*
KELLER *fastens the napkin around* HELEN'S *neck;
she permits it.*)

There. It's not unnatural, most of us take some
aversion to our teachers, and occasionally another
hand can smooth things out.

(*He puts a fork in* HELEN'S *hand;* HELEN *takes it.
Genially:*)

Now. Shall we start all over?

(*He goes back around the table, and sits.* ANNIE
stands watching. HELEN *is motionless, thinking things
through, until with a wicked glee she deliberately
flings the fork on the floor. After another moment
she plunges her hand into her food, and crams a fistful into her mouth.*)

JAMES [WEARILY]: I think we've started all over—

> (KELLER *shoots a glare at him, as* HELEN *plunges her other hand into* ANNIE'S *plate.* ANNIE *at once moves in, to grasp her wrist, and* HELEN *flinging out a hand encounters the pitcher; she swings with it at* ANNIE; ANNIE *falling back blocks it with an elbow, but the water flies over her dress.* ANNIE *gets her breath, then snatches the pitcher away in one hand, hoists* HELEN *up bodily under the other arm, and starts to carry her out, kicking.* KELLER *stands.*)

ANNIE [SAVAGELY POLITE]: Don't get up!
KELLER: Where are you going?
ANNIE: Don't smooth anything else out for me, don't interfere in any way! I treat her like a seeing child because I *ask* her to see, I *expect* her to see, don't undo what I do!
KELLER: Where are you taking her?
ANNIE: To make her fill this pitcher again!

> (She *thrusts out with* HELEN *under her arm, but* HELEN *escapes up the stairs and* ANNIE *runs after her.* KELLER *stands rigid.* AUNT EV *is astounded.*)

AUNT EV: You let her speak to you like that, Arthur? A creature who *works* for you?
KELLER [ANGRILY]: No. I don't.

> (He *is starting after* ANNIE *when* JAMES, *on his feet with shaky resolve, interposes his chair between them in* KELLER'S *path.*)

JAMES: Let her go.
KELLER: What!
JAMES [A SWALLOW]: I said—let her go. She's right.

> (KELLER *glares at the chair and him.* JAMES *takes a deep breath, then headlong:*)

She's right, Kate's right, I'm right, and you're wrong.
If you drive her away from here it will be over my
dead—chair, has it never occurred to you that on
one occasion you might be consummately wrong?

(KELLER's *stare is unbelieving, even a little fascinated.*
KATE *rises in trepidation, to mediate.*)

KATE: Captain.

(KELLER *stops her with his raised hand; his eyes stay
on* JAMES' *pale face, for a long hold. When he finally
finds his voice, it is gruff.*)

KELLER: Sit down, everyone.

(*He sits.* KATE *sits.* JAMES *holds onto his chair.*
KELLER *speaks mildly.*)

Please sit down, Jimmie.

(JAMES *sits, and a moveless silence prevails;* KELLER's
eyes do not leave him.

ANNIE *has pulled* HELEN *downstairs again by one
hand, the pitcher in her other hand, down the porch
steps, and across the yard to the pump. She puts*
HELEN's *hand on the pump handle, grimly.*)

ANNIE: All right. Pump.

(HELEN *touches her cheek, waits uncertainly.*)

No, she's not here. Pump!

(*She forces* HELEN's *hand to work the handle, then
lets go. And* HELEN *obeys. She pumps till the water
comes, then* ANNIE *puts the pitcher in her other hand
and guides it under the spout, and the water tumbling*

half into and half around the pitcher douses HELEN's
hand. ANNIE *takes over the handle to keep water
coming, and does automatically what she has done so
many times before, spells into* HELEN's *free palm:*)

Water. W, a, t, e, r. Water. It has a—*name*—

(*And now the miracle happens.* HELEN *drops the
pitcher on the slab under the spout, it shatters. She
stands transfixed.* ANNIE *freezes on the pump handle:
there is a change in the sundown light, and with it
a change in* HELEN's *face, some light coming into it
we have never seen there, some struggle in the depths
behind it; and her lips tremble, trying to remember
something the muscles around them once knew, till at
last it finds its way out, painfully, a baby sound buried
under the debris of years of dumbness.*)

HELEN: Wah. Wah.

(*And again, with great effort*)

Wah. Wah.

(HELEN *plunges her hand into the dwindling water,
spells into her own palm. Then she gropes frantically,*
ANNIE *reaches for her hand, and* HELEN *spells into*
ANNIE's *hand.*)

ANNIE [WHISPERING]: Yes.

(HELEN *spells into it again.*)

Yes!

(HELEN *grabs at the handle, pumps for more water,
plunges her hand into its spurt and grabs* ANNIE's
to spell it again.)

Yes! Oh, my dear—

(She falls to her knees to clasp HELEN's *hand, but* HELEN *pulls it free, stands almost bewildered, then drops to the ground, pats it swiftly, holds up her palm, imperious.* ANNIE *spells into it:)*

Ground.

*(*HELEN *spells it back.)*

Yes!

*(*HELEN *whirls to the pump, pats it, holds up her palm, and* ANNIE *spells into it.)*

Pump.

*(*HELEN *spells it back.)*

Yes! Yes!

(Now HELEN *is in such an excitement she is possessed, wild, trembling, cannot be still, turns, runs, falls on the porch steps, claps it, reaches out her palm, and* ANNIE *is at it instantly to spell:)*

Step.

*(*HELEN *has no time to spell back now, she whirls groping, to touch anything, encounters the trellis, shakes it, thrusts out her palm, and* ANNIE *while spelling to her cries wildly at the house.)*

Trellis. Mrs. Keller! *Mrs. Keller!*

(Inside, KATE *starts to her feet.* HELEN *scrambles back onto the porch, groping, and finds the bell*

*string, tugs it; the bell rings, the distant chimes begin
tolling the hour, all the bells in town seem to break
into speech while* HELEN *reaches out and* ANNIE *spells
feverishly into her hand.* KATE *hurries out, with* KELLER
after her; AUNT EV *is on her feet, to peer out the
window; only* JAMES *remains at the table, and with
a napkin wipes his damp brow. From up right and
left the servants—*VINEY, *the two Negro children, the
other servant—run in, and stand watching from a distance as* HELEN, *ringing the bell, with her other hand
encounters her mother's skirt; when she throws a hand
out,* ANNIE *spells into it:)*

Mother.

*(*KELLER *now seizes* HELEN'S *hand, she touches him,
gestures a hand, and* ANNIE *again spells:)*

Papa— She *knows!*

*(*KATE *and* KELLER *go to their knees, stammering,
clutching* HELEN *to them, and* ANNIE *steps unsteadily
back to watch the threesome,* HELEN *spelling wildly
into* KATE'S *hand, then into* KELLER'S, KATE *spelling
back into* HELEN'S; *they cannot keep their hands off
her, and rock her in their clasp.*

Then HELEN *gropes, feels nothing, turns all around,
pulls free, and comes with both hands groping, to
find* ANNIE. *She encounters* ANNIE'S *thighs,* ANNIE
kneels to her, HELEN'S *hand pats* ANNIE'S *cheek impatiently, points a finger, and waits; and* ANNIE *spells
into it:)*

Teacher.

*(*HELEN *spells it back, slowly;* ANNIE *nods.)*

Teacher.

(She holds HELEN's *hand to her cheek. Presently* HELEN *withdraws it, not jerkily, only with reserve, and retreats a step. She stands thinking it over, then turns again and stumbles back to her parents. They try to embrace her, but she has something else in mind, it is to get the keys, and she hits* KATE's *pocket until* KATE *digs them out for her.*

ANNIE *with her own load of emotion has retreated, her back turned, toward the pump, to sit;* KATE *moves to* HELEN, *touches her hand questioningly, and* HELEN *spells a word to her.* KATE *comprehends it, their first act of verbal communication, and she can hardly utter the word aloud, in wonder, gratitude, and deprivation; it is a moment in which she simultaneously finds and loses a child.)*

KATE: Teacher?

*(*ANNIE *turns; and* KATE, *facing* HELEN *in her direction by the shoulders, holds her back, holds her back, and then relinquishes her.* HELEN *feels her way across the yard, rather shyly, and when her moving hands touch* ANNIE's *skirt she stops. Then she holds out the keys and places them in* ANNIE's *hand. For a moment neither of them moves. Then* HELEN *slides into* ANNIE's *arms, and lifting away her smoked glasses, kisses her on the cheek.* ANNIE *gathers her in.*

KATE *torn both ways turns from this, gestures the servants off, and makes her way into the house, on* KELLER's *arm. The servants go, in separate directions.*

The lights are half down now, except over the pump. ANNIE *and* HELEN *are here, alone in the yard.* ANNIE *has found* HELEN's *hand, almost without knowing it, and she spells slowly into it, her voice unsteady, whispering:)*

ANNIE: I, love, Helen.

(She clutches the child to her, tight this time, not spelling, whispering into her hair.)

Forever, and—

(She stops. The lights over the pump are taking on the color of the past, and it brings ANNIE's *head up, her eyes opening, in fear; and as slowly as though drawn she rises, to listen, with her hand on* HELEN's *shoulders. She waits, waits, listening with ears and eyes both, slowly here, slowly there: and hears only silence. There are no voices. The color passes on, and when her eyes come back to* HELEN *she can breathe the end of her phrase without fear:)*

—ever.

(In the family room KATE *has stood over the table, staring at* HELEN's *plate, with* KELLER *at her shoulder; now* JAMES *takes a step to move her chair in, and* KATE *sits, with head erect, and* KELLER *inclines his head to* JAMES; *so it is* AUNT EV, *hesitant, and rather humble, who moves to the door.*

Outside HELEN *tugs at* ANNIE's *hand, and* ANNIE *comes with it.* HELEN *pulls her toward the house; and hand in hand, they cross the yard, and ascend the porch steps, in the rising lights, to where* AUNT EV *is holding the door open for them.*

The curtain ends the play.)